Discover
Seeds of Change

SCIENCE WEEKLY

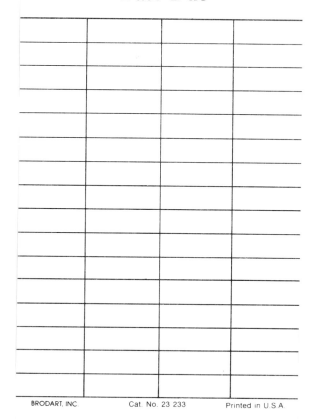

Date Due

Menlo Park, California • Reading, Massachusetts • New York
Don Mills, Ontario • Wokingham, England • Amsterdam • Bonn
Sydney • Singapore • Tokyo • Madrid • San Juan • Paris
Seoul • Milan • Mexico City • Taipei

Contents

This book is published by Innovative Learning™, an imprint of Addison-Wesley's Alternative Publishing Group.

This material is based on "Seeds of Change," the quincentennial commemoration of Columbus's voyages to America. The "Seeds of Change" research, exhibitions, publications, and programs have been made possible through the support of the Xerox Corporation. Development of *Seeds of Change* educational materials has been a cooperative venture with the National Museum of Natural History, Smithsonian Institution; Science Weekly, Inc.; and the National Council for the Social Studies.

ISBN 0-201-49003-X

1 2 3 4 5 6 7 8 9 10-ML-98 97 96 95 94 93

Sailing the Ocean Blue

In 1492 Christopher Columbus sailed west across the Atlantic Ocean. Columbus had studied **geography** and knew the earth was round. He was looking for a shorter route to the Indies. Instead he reached the Americas. The world was much larger than the geographers knew.

First Voyage

Columbus made the first voyage to the Americas in three small wooden ships. **Sailing ships** were much improved by this time. They had stronger hulls and improved sails. They were now more responsive to shifts in the weather. Improvements in ships and the invention of scientific **instruments** made longer ocean voyages possible. This opened an age of great discovery.

quadrant

hourglass

compass

Navigation

Columbus was both a **scientist** and a sailor. His knowledge of **astronomy** and geography also made him an outstanding **navigator**. His ships had the most up-to-date instruments available at the time. Columbus used the **quadrant** to figure out his ship's position. He used the **compass** to find direction. Columbus often used the method of **dead reckoning** to determine his ship's location. This method combined an estimate of the ship's distance and speed, plus the navigator's knowledge of the sea.

Many sailors were restless during the voyage. A long trip into unknown waters frightened them. At one point, the ships drifted into still water in the Atlantic Ocean. The water was almost solid with seaweed, which ocean currents had brought there. The frightened sailors named the area "Sargasso" which means "sea plant."

Log

Columbus wrote down what happened each day and what he saw. He was one of the first sailors to keep a ship's **log** or journal. The log tells us that on October 12, 1492, the crew landed on a small island. They found people different from any they had ever seen. Columbus named the island San Salvador. He called the people Indians because he thought he was in India.

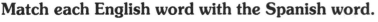 Vocabulary

Columbus was born in Italy, but he always wrote in Spanish.
Match each English word with the Spanish word.

1.	ship	a.	papa
2.	sail	b.	tierra
3.	land	c.	barco
4.	treasures	d.	navegar
5.	corn	e.	tesoros
6.	potato	f.	maiz
7.	sugar	g.	caballo
8.	horse	h.	azucar

Weekly Lab

Let's make a quadrant!

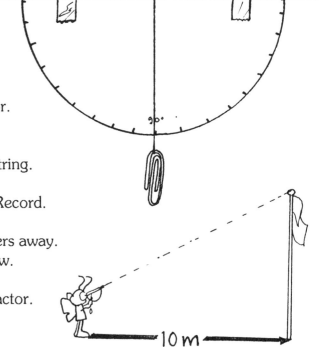

> **You need:** protractor, plastic straw, string, tape, paper clip, meter stick, scissors

Step 1: Tape the straw to the back of the protractor.

Step 2: Tie the string to the middle of the straw. Tie the paper clip to the other end of the string.

Step 3: Measure your height with the meter stick. Record.

Step 4: Locate a tall object outside. Stand 10 meters away. Sight the top of the object through the straw.

Step 5: Pinch the string where it touches the protractor. Record the degree mark.

You will use your data in the Weekly Problem.

❓ Weekly Problem

Construct an angle at F that equals the degrees you measured with your quadrant. Make sure the angle at L is 90 degrees. Divide your height in cm by 100. Extend line YL by this number in cm. Measure YW. Multiply by 100. This is the height in meters of your tall object.

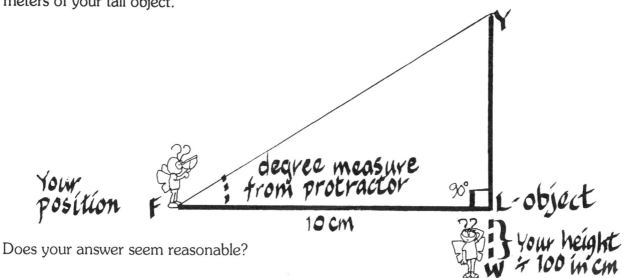

Does your answer seem reasonable?

Writing for Science

You are a crew member on Columbus's ship.
Write a journal entry for the day you first go ashore.
How do you feel? What do you see?

 Challenge

Plan a trip from your home to San Salvador. Use a map to find the map scale for distance. Answer the questions below.

1. Mark your route. What places will you pass through?

2. Approximately how many miles is your trip? How long will it take you?

3. What will be your method of transportation? What will it cost?

4. What scientific instruments will be used?

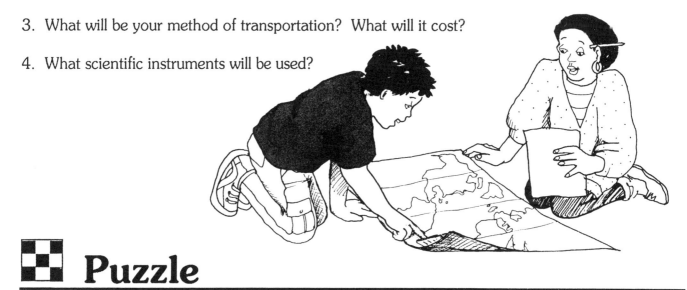

Puzzle

"Navegar" is the Spanish word for "to sail." Can you think of other English words that are similar to the Spanish words in Vocabulary? (For example, "navegar" is similar to "navigate.") See who can think of the most words.

A-Maizing Corn

If you think corn is an all-American food, you're right! Corn, or **maize**, was first grown by Native Americans! It grew in **Mesoamerica**, the area we now call Mexico and Central America, thousands of years before Columbus arrived.

The people of ancient Mesoamerica spent their time wandering from place to place, searching for wild berries and seeds to eat. Some of the seeds were from wild grasses. One day, the people tried planting these grass seeds. They probably chose the biggest and best seeds for planting. Eventually they grew plants like our present day corn. Imagine how the people felt! At last there was plenty to eat!

How Corn Was Used

Some corn was eaten fresh, but most was dried, sorted by color, and stacked for later use. The women soaked the hard dry corn in water and wood ashes, then ground the softened kernels into cornmeal for making bread and **porridge**. They even made corn drinks and popped popcorn!

Not all corn was eaten. Dried **kernels** were used as beads and as markers in games. Medicines were made from the silk, and corn cobs were used as fuel for fires. **Husks** were woven into mats and baskets. Stalks were chewed for their sweet taste. Nothing was wasted!

Groups of people settled near the growing corn. Settlements became villages and some villages became large cities. People to the north, in what is now the United States, began to grow corn, too. Throughout the area, native people grew many kinds of corn. Corn was the most important grain of **pre-Columbian** Americans! It became their gift to the rest of the world!

Ceremonies and Customs

Special **ceremonies** surrounded the growing of corn. People told ancient **myths** about the Corn Spirits. Some tribes sprinkled sacred cornmeal on their fields so the corn would grow. When the first ear of corn was harvested the Hopis thanked the Corn Spirits by sharing it with them. To Native Americans, corn meant life!

 Vocabulary

"Pre" is a prefix that means "before."

Match each definition with the correct word.

1. the time before recorded history

2. existing beforehand

3. made beforehand

4. happening before Columbus arrived in America

prefabricated

pre-Columbian

prehistoric

preexisting

How many other words can you think of that begin with "pre?"

Weekly Lab

Why did ancient Americans soak corn?

You need: some corn kernels, 2 rocks, 4 pieces of paper, 4 plastic cups, water

Step 1: Label the cups 1-4. Divide the seeds evenly into the cups.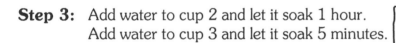

Step 2: Add water to cup 1 and let it soak overnight.

Step 3: Add water to cup 2 and let it soak 1 hour.
Add water to cup 3 and let it soak 5 minutes.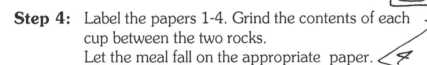

Step 4: Label the papers 1-4. Grind the contents of each cup between the two rocks.
Let the meal fall on the appropriate paper.

Step 5: Try to make balls with each type of ground meal.

How did soaking affect the grinding?

![icon] Weekly Problem

The ancient Mayans invented a system for writing numbers.
Each dot (●) equaled 1 and each dash (—) equaled 5.

Use Mayan numbers to count the number of ears of corn in each stack.

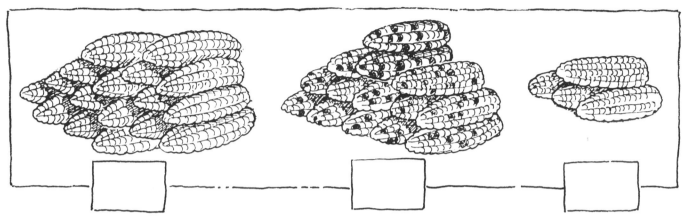

Bonus: You need 19 ears of each kind of corn. How many more ears of each must you harvest?
Write your calculations in Mayan numbers.

![icon] Writing for Science

Listen to the Pueblo myth about the Corn Maidens. **Work in groups to invent a myth to explain something about your school. Draw a codex to illustrate your myth.**

Challenge

You are part of an archaeological team, digging in Bat Cave, New Mexico. You are about to uncover some exciting evidence!

You find many corn cobs. As you dig down into the more ancient layers, the corn cobs become smaller and smaller. What can you tell about the people who once lived here? What other items would you look for?

Puzzle

Native Americans had many different words for corn. One of them was mahiz, or maize.
Decode the message to discover what maize meant to ancient Americans!

1. Change the Mayan numbers to Arabic numbers, the numbers you use every day.
2. Use the table below to decode the message.

Growing Corn

Imagine over 500 seeds on just one ear of corn! Each seed can grow into a plant with two or three ears of corn. Think of how many people these ears could feed! Native Americans shared this gift of life with the early settlers and traders in America. The traders sent the corn seeds back to Europe. Today, over 200 million people worldwide depend on corn as their main food.

Native Americans discovered that corn grew better when planted with beans and squash. Beans made the soil more fertile. Squash kept soil damp and prevented weeds. Some gardeners still use these Native American ways. But, large farms use chemical **fertilizers** instead of beans to improve the soil. They also use power machines to plant and harvest. Now farmers can harvest 150 bushels in the time it took the early settlers to harvest one!

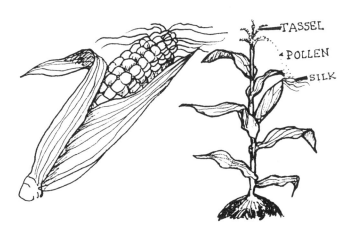

Food from Sunshine

Unlike humans, plants make their own food. This process is called **photosynthesis**. Leaves capture the energy of the sun and turn it into food energy. This food helps cornstalks grow. Extra food is stored in the plump **kernels** we eat.

Pollination

A fully grown cornstalk has a feathery **tassel**. Pollen from a tassel must fall on the silk of an ear before seeds can form on the cob.

How are new kinds of corn developed? Farmers take pollen from one type of corn and put it on the **silks** of another type. The corn that results will be a little like each parent plant. Scientists are trying to pass on the qualities that make Hopi corn grow in the southwestern desert to other types of corn. Perhaps this new corn will grow in parts of the world where there is little rain.

The Right Seed

Where will new types grow best? How will they be used? Farmers grow test fields of the corn to answer these questions. Over many generations of selecting the best seeds, corn has been developed that is sweeter, pops better, or has heavier, more nutritious ears. Does corn grow where you live? What kind?

🅰️ Vocabulary

Read the sentences. Circle whether the bold word is a noun or a verb.

1. Corn seeds **store** food.
    noun   verb

2. Corn is sold at the grocery **store**.
    noun   vorb

3. A seed contains a baby **plant**.
    noun   verb

4. The farmer will **plant** 20 acres this year.
    noun   verb

5. How can fuel made with corn **power** that tractor?
    noun   verb

6. Eating corn gives people **power**.
    noun   verb

Find other words on the front page that can be used as a noun or verb. Share your examples.

Ⓜ️ Weekly Lab

What conditions are best for growing popcorn seeds?

> **You need:** presoaked popcorn kernels (overnight), water, tablespoon, 4 clear cups (labelled wet/cold, wet/warm, dry/cold, dry/warm), paper towels, marking pen, millimeter ruler, refrigerator, thermometer

Work in teams.

Step 1: Put 2 cm of water in "wet" cups.

Step 2: Put 5 seeds between crumpled towel and sides of each cup.

Step 3: Predict which seeds will grow best.
Keep "cold" cups in refrigerator.

Step 4: Keep a daily log for one week to record temperature, sprouting, length of roots, and height of leaves under different conditions.

Step 5: Put a dot of indelible ink on a root as it emerges.

Step 6: Predict whether roots grow at the seed or tip.

Were your predictions correct?
Which conditions do these seeds like?

Weekly Problem

Use rounded numbers in the table to complete the bar graph.

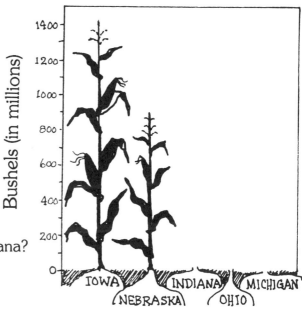

State	Bushels (in millions)	Rounded
Iowa	1,445	1400
Nebraska	852	900
Indiana	691	
Ohio	342	
Michigan	222	

Answer the questions using your graph.

1. How much corn did Iowa grow?
2. How much more did Nebraska produce than Indiana?
3. Did Indiana, Ohio, and Michigan together grow more or less than Iowa?
4. How much would Ohio need to increase production to equal Nebraska?

 # Writing for Science

Imagine yourself an early settler. What have you learned about corn? Write a letter to a friend in Europe. Describe how corn tastes, how the plant looks, and how to grow it.

 # Challenge

Answer the questions. Use an atlas if necessary.

1. Identify these states.

2. Which states grow corn?

3. Which states have corn and hogs?

4. Which state has corn, but not hogs or tools?

5. Which state grows the most corn?

Hint: It has hogs. It touches Wisconsin.

 # Puzzle

Corn belongs to the grass family of plants. **Fill in the blanks to show where tulip, pine, wheat, Tree, and daisy belong. Name some other members of these families.**

PLANTS

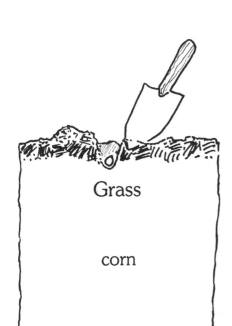

Grass

corn

Flower

oak

Corn Today

What do chewing gum, tires, fireworks, and vitamin pills have in common? Corn is used to make each one of them!

Most of us have eaten popcorn, corn-on-the-cob, and corn bread. Some of us know that corn is fed to livestock, too. But you might be surprised to find out that corn is hidden in hundreds of other things we use every day!

Think of corn as a treasure. That treasure is unlocked by **corn refining technology**. Here's how it happens. When it arrives at the corn refining plant, the corn is washed. Next it is soaked and ground to break the kernels apart. Then each part of the kernel is **processed**, or changed.

Starch, or **endosperm**, is the most important part of the kernel. Starch looks like a simple, white powder, but it's the starting material for a great number and variety of products. It's not only in cookies, breads, and microwaveable dinners, it's also used to make batteries, crayons, paper, and glue. Thanks to starch, there's good news for the environment, too. Starch-based **biodegradable** plastics are beginning to replace some **petroleum**-based plastics. Can you think of ways this will help the world around us?

Some starch is changed into sugars and syrups. You'll find **corn syrup** in fruit drinks and chewing gum as well as ketchup and peanut butter. Corn syrup is also used to make shoe polish, paper, and explosives! And that's not all. A sugar called **dextrose** is **fermented** to make **ethanol**, a cleaner burning fuel for cars. This sugar is like the sugar in your blood. Doctors feed it to patients who are too sick to eat. Corn is a life saver, too.

Another part of the kernel, the **germ**, is pressed to get corn oil. You're right if you'd expect to find corn oil in margarine and salad dressing. But did you know that it's also used to produce paints and **insecticides**?

Nothing is wasted. The leftover parts of the kernel are made into nutritious animal feed. So, even a hamburger has corn hidden in it. Corn is an American treasure!

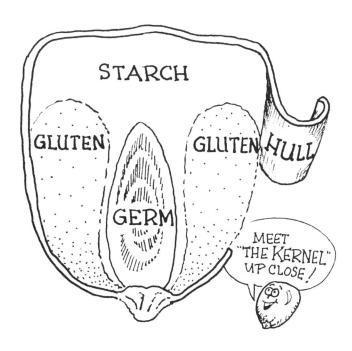

⟨c⟩ Vocabulary

Corn is found in many foods. **Read these ingredient labels. Choose the product.**
The first one is done for you.

1. **Ingredients:** water, liquid corn oil, partially hydrogenated corn oil, whey, gelatin, salt, beta carotene
   a) corn bread   (b) margarine)

2. **Ingredients:** stone ground corn, peanut oil
   a) tortilla chips   b) salad dressing

3. **Ingredients:** sugar, cornstarch, salt, soybean oil, nonfat milk
   a) pudding   b) canned fruit

4. **Ingredients:** carbonated water, high fructose corn syrup, citric acid, and natural flavors
   a) chewing gum   b) soft drink

Bonus: Look for corn, corn syrup, cornstarch, and corn oil on ingredient labels of your food.

⟨H⟩ Weekly Lab

What can you make when you mix cornstarch and water?

You need: cornstarch, container of water, bowl, spoon, straw, or medicine dropper

Step 1:   Measure out 1 spoon of cornstarch.
Step 2:   Guess the drops of water needed to make two products.
   Product 1: Forms a solid.
   Product 2: Drips from fingers, yet solid when pressed.
   Record your guess.
Step 3:   After making the first product, do you want to revise your prediction of how much water the second product needs?
Step 4:   Record your observations.

⟨⟩ Weekly Problem

This graph shows how refined corn was used in 1989.
Answer the questions.

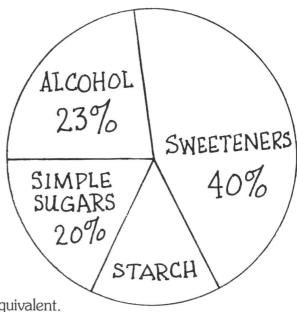

TOTAL = 960 MILLION BUSHELS

ALCOHOL 23%

SWEETENERS 40%

SIMPLE SUGARS 20%

STARCH

1. What is the greatest use for refined corn?
2. Simple sugars were 1/5 of the total and alcohol was about 1/4.   Which is more?
3. Sweeteners were 2/5 of the total. Write a decimal equivalent.
4. What percent was used to make starch?

CROP YEAR 1989

Writing for Science

Cornstarch has been used to make biodegradable products like plastic bags and packing foam. Work in teams. **Choose a product and design a label. Write a 30 second radio or TV ad explaining why people should use biodegradable products.**

CORN CAN MAKE A WORLD OF DIFFERENCE FOR OUR WORLD!

◫ Challenge

Find the commodity prices for corn in the financial pages of the newspaper.
How much would 5,000 bushels cost? What would your profit be if you bought 5,000 bushels last year?

▦ Puzzle

Find more corn products in this Word Search.

```
F R O S T I N G L U E
I L A K B U L U O I P
R I N K A M P M E A T
E C E J T S O A P A L
W O E A T O C H A L K
O R P M E D I C I N E
R I T I R E S O N I R
K C A S I M O N T S E
S E S H E R B E R T N
M A R T S T R A W S T
```

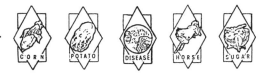

The Potato Conquers Europe

Potatoes began their journey around the world when Spanish **explorers** came to South America. Francisco Pizarro was looking for gold when he came across the Incas in Peru in the 1500s. He found that the people were very skilled in **agriculture**. They grew many food crops that had not been seen in Europe. More importantly, they were able to store enough food to feed their population for years.

The Potato Travels to Europe

Pizarro and his sailors took some of these strange new plants to Spain. Besides the potato, Pizarro and other explorers probably carried corn, sweet potatoes, tomatoes, peanuts, chili peppers, and pineapples to their European ports.

The potato is a fat, **underground** stem called a **tuber**. At first, many Europeans did not want to eat the potato because it grew in the ground. They fed the potato to their farm animals. Potatoes proved to be an excellent food for the livestock, and the animals thrived.

In the 1600 and 1700s, constant wars in Europe forced people to take another look at the potato. When a conquering army marched through a country, soldiers would burn all the buildings and destroy all the food. However, the potato tubers lay hidden in the ground, so they were left alone. The people had to eat them to keep from starving. They soon found that potatoes were a very good food for humans as well as animals.

The Potato Comes to North America

Potatoes spread north from Spain through France and into Northern Europe, and then to England and Ireland. In the early 1600s, people in England shipped the potato to Bermuda. A few years later potatoes were sent to the Jamestown colony in Virginia. Potatoes did not become popular in North America until the **settlers** brought them from Europe beginning in the 1800s. Thomas Jefferson made the potato more popular by serving french fries in the White House. Today, people all over the world enjoy the potato and its many dishes.

![icon] Vocabulary

Make each word plural.

potato   tomato   burro   echo

hero   rodeo   yo-yo   hello

![icon] Weekly Lab

Can you think of other irregular plurals?

What is a good way to grow the most potatoes?

You need: two potatoes (one whole and one cut up with an eye on each piece), several large pots, soil

Step 1:   Plant the whole potato in one of the pots. Label.
Step 2:   Plant each potato piece in a separate pot.
              Make sure the eye is sticking up. Label each pot.
Step 3:   Place all the pots in the same sunny spot.
Step 4:   Keep the soil in each pot moist but not wet.
              Record the height of each plant each day until the
              plants are about 10 centimeters tall.

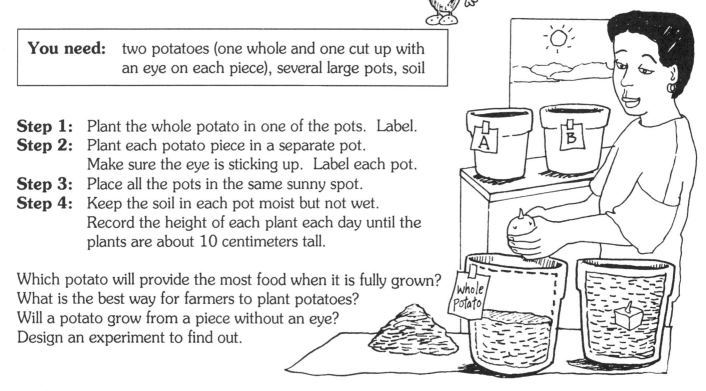

Which potato will provide the most food when it is fully grown?
What is the best way for farmers to plant potatoes?
Will a potato grow from a piece without an eye?
Design an experiment to find out.

Weekly Problem

The distance from Peru to Spain is about 5150 miles.
The distance from Spain to England is about 770 miles.
The distance from England to Bermuda is about 4700 miles.

Which is farthest?

How far did the potato travel in all?

Bonus: Can you find a city that is the same round trip distance from your home?

Writing for Science

In 18th century France, Antoine-Auguste Parmentier invited Benjamin Franklin to an all potato meal to introduce him to the tuber. **Write a letter to Franklin inviting him to the meal. Describe some of the dishes.**

Challenge

Label each statement as fact or opinion.

Farm animals loved the taste of potatoes. _____

The potato is an underground stem. _____

The potato tastes best when it is baked. _____

Foods that grow underground are bad for you. _____

The potato came to Europe from South America. _____

Puzzle

Jack has a "magic garden." He has 16 potato plants in 4 rows of 4. The total number of potatoes from each row and from each column is 24. **Fill in the missing numbers.**

2		8	
10	2		7
			5
8	8	2	

Potatoes Today

Potatoes are good to eat and they're good for you, too! After slow acceptance in Europe, they have become one of the world's favorite foods. Potatoes are grown and eaten in more than 130 countries. Almost every country has its own potato specialty. In fast food restaurants around the world, American fries are making the potato even more popular.

The Almost Perfect Food

What makes the potato so good for you? The potato is an almost perfect food. More than 15% of the weight of the potato is **carbohydrates**. Carbohydrates give you long-term energy. The potato is also low in **calories** and fat content. The average potato has only 110 calories. A baked or boiled potato has almost no fat. Of course, many people put butter or sour cream on a baked potato. French fries absorb some fat from cooking oil. Potato salad has fat from mayonnaise.

Potatoes are second only to the orange as a source of vitamin C. Sea captains may have known this when they fed potatoes to their crews to keep them from getting scurvy. Potatoes also contain many other important **vitamins** and **minerals** that help you grow and remain strong.

Potatoes in the Future

Scientists continue to experiment with the potato. They are working to develop a **true potato seed (TPS)** that will be as reliable as potato eyes for growing uniform potatoes. It takes almost 2,000 kilograms of tubers to plant about 2.5 acres. Imagine how much easier it would be to plant this area with a handful of seeds! Scientists are also working on a high **protein** potato that will grow in developing countries. It's even being considered as a staple crop for farms in outer space!

More Than a Food

Potatoes are used for other things besides food. They can be used to make fuel, medicines, paper, and **biodegradable** plastics. They make starch and adhesives and are important in dyes. They are even used in waste water treatment. What common ingredient do potatoes and corn share that makes them so versatile?

🔊 Vocabulary

Use the words in the chart to identify each statement.

1. These nutrients are made of sugar and starch. They provide long term energy.
2. These nutrients are essential for building and repairing tissues. They are made up of amino acids.
3. This mineral helps build muscle tissues.
4. This mineral helps make strong bones.
5. These are chemical elements needed for good health.
6. These are substances needed for normal growth and health. They are often named with letters.

🎵 Weekly Lab

The potato is a source of energy.
That energy can be converted into different forms.

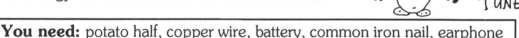

You need: potato half, copper wire, battery, common iron nail, earphone

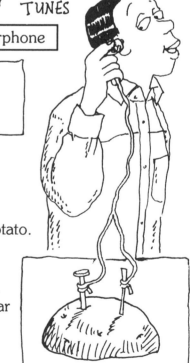

Step 1: Stick two pieces of copper wire into the potato half about an inch apart.

Step 2: Attach the other ends to a battery. What happens? (A gas shows there is a chemical reaction.)

Step 3: Disconnect the battery. Take one of the wires out of the potato. Stick the nail in its place.

Step 4: Attach one end of the earphone wire to the nail. Attach the other end to the scraped end of the copper wire.

Step 5: Use the earphone to listen to the potato. The static you hear is current flowing through the potato.

Can you "listen" to other foods? (Hint: Try a lemon.)

❓ Weekly Problem

About 3 kilograms of potatoes supply enough calories for an adult for one day.
The average adult eats enough kilograms of potatoes each year to provide calories for 20 days.
Use these facts to calculate the number of kilograms of potatoes the average adult eats in one year.

🔺 Writing for Science

Write a newspaper article about the importance of the potato in the future. Why is the true potato seed important? What will the high protein potato mean for people in developing countries?

⊟ Challenge

Design a new potato product that uses the energy you heard and saw in the **Weekly Lab.** Could you use the electrical energy in the potato like a battery?

▩ Puzzle

Across

1. snack or oil, native to America
2. guacamole ingredient, native to America
3. made from cane or beets, very popular
4. native American food adopted by Italians for sauces

Down

5. freeze-dried potato
6. source of flavor, found in chocolate, orginally used as money
7. staff of life for ancient Mesoamericans
8. near perfect food

Microconquistadors

Explorers entering the Americas in the 1400s brought weapons to conquer the Native Americans. However, they did not realize that their ultimate weapon would not be their guns but **disease**. Diseases such as smallpox, measles, and diphtheria arrived with the Europeans and rapidly killed large numbers of Native Americans. In some cases, whole populations were wiped out. These diseases spread so rapidly that many natives died before ever seeing a European.

The Exchange of Disease

Many European children died from infectious diseases. The ones who survived the illnesses and grew to adulthood developed **immunity**. Immunity means that a person will not get sick if exposed to a specific disease. The soldiers who came to America were the lucky survivors of these diseases and developed immunity. However, in many cases the soldiers were still **carriers**. They could give the disease to others.

America was not free of disease when Columbus arrived. However, the natives had no immunity from the diseases brought from Europe. This is the reason so many died.

Immunity

Building immunity begins when disease-causing **microbes**, or **germs**, enter the body. **White blood cells** fight the germs and destroy them. Then the body makes special cells called **memory cells** to remember that type of germ. If that type of germ ever enters the body again, the memory cells recognize it and destroy it very quickly.

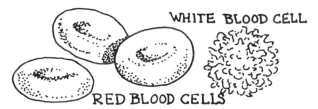

WHITE BLOOD CELL

RED BLOOD CELLS

Vaccines are now given to help the body build immunity to infectious disease. You get a vaccine either as a shot or as a liquid to drink. Each vaccine causes the body to develop memory cells for a specific germ.

Children in the United States should be vaccinated for measles, mumps, rubella, whooping cough, tetanus, diptheria, polio, and the HIB virus before starting school. People who do not get the required vaccinations may become ill if exposed to any of the germs. Recently, there have been several serious outbreaks of measles. These outbreaks could have been avoided if everyone had gotten the required **immunizations**. Make sure you are immunized.

We can only wonder what might have happened if Native Americans had been immune to European diseases. These tiny germs were able to change the course of history.

Vocabulary

Fill in the blanks.

Use the circled letters to find the secret word.

SECRET WORD
◯ ◯ ◯ ◯ ◯

1. prevents a person from getting some types of germs Ⓞ __ __ __ __ __ __

2. another word for vaccination Ⓘ __ __ __ __ __ __ __ __ __ __

3. infectious microbes __ __ Ⓔ __ __ __

4. process of fighting germs in the body __ __ __ Ⓞ __ __ __ __

5. organisms which cannot be seen with naked eye __ __ __ __ __ __ __ Ⓞ

Bonus: Use a dictionary to write a definition of the secret word.

Weekly Lab

How do infections spread?

> **You need:** grid with 1/2" squares, cup of beans

Step 1: Each bean represents a person who has infectious germs.
The squares on the grid represent healthy people.
Drop one bean onto the paper grid. How many squares in
the grid does the bean touch?

Step 2: Take the same number of beans out of the bean cup as the
number of squares that were touched in step 1. These beans
represent newly infected people.

Step 3: Drop all the beans in your hand onto the paper grid.
How many squares in the grid did the beans touch?

Step 4: Take from the cup as many beans as squares touched
in the last step. Drop all of these beans onto the grid.
How many squares in the grid did the beans touch?

Step 5: Repeat step 4. How many squares in the grid did the
beans touch?

What did you find out about infectious diseases?
How can you stop infections from spreading rapidly?

♔ Weekly Problem

If a germ divides into two germs every 30 minutes, how many germs would there be after 1 hour (60 minutes)? After 2 hours (120 minutes)?

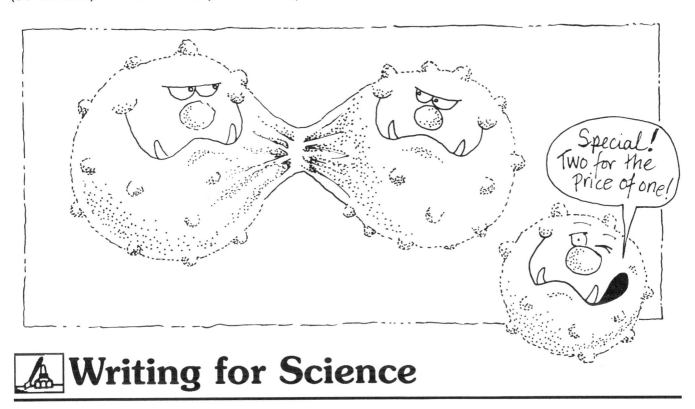

⚠ Writing for Science

Write several paragraphs to show how history might have been different if so many Native Americans had not died from European diseases.

⊞ Challenge

The following are Joyce's results for the Weekly Lab.

Plot the results on the graph.

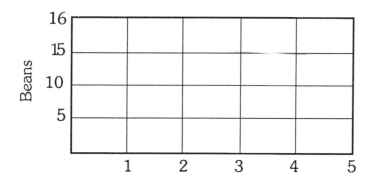

Number of drops

Results	
Drop	Bean
1	2
2	4
3	8
4	16

How many beans do you think you would have after 5 drops?
Explain your answer.

▦ Puzzle

Can you find the name of some of the diseases you are vaccinated for?

Start at the arrow and go down.

Write down every other letter.

```
      M U U S
    N         M
    S         M
    A         P
    E         E
    T         S
      L E S T A
```

Cures and Carriers

Like all living things, germs need food, moisture, and a warm place to live. The human body is the perfect home for many germs. We can be **infected** by germs in food, water, or by contact with certain animals and insects.

Disease Carriers

At the time of Columbus's voyage in 1492, garbage and human wastes were dumped into the streets of European cities. This allowed disease **microbes,** or germs, to **contaminate** the drinking water. Rats roamed the streets carrying bubonic plague from house to house. Cows grazed on infected grass and passed tuberculosis to humans in their milk. These diseases and their carriers traveled with the explorers to America. **Malaria**, carried only by a certain mosquito, found a carrier once it got to America.

Smallpox was the worst disease to come to America. Millions of Native Americans got sick and died because they had no immunity. Because of the lack of immunity, **epidemics** spread across the land and killed entire groups of Native Americans. It was 300 years before a cure was found. By then, it was too late.

Cures

Cures for some diseases came from Native American healers. For example, Aztec doctors identified more than 1,200 plants that helped treat disease. South American natives showed the Europeans how to make "fever tea" from the bark of the **chinchona** (sin-KO-na) tree. The tea contained quinine which treated malaria and other diseases.

European explorers knew there were many useful medicines in America and they took some of them back to Europe. Today, scientists continue to find cures for diseases in the plants found in American forests.

Disease Prevention

Because we now know how germs spread, we can protect ourselves from diseases. The government purifies our water, inspects our food, and processes our wastes in sewage treatment plants. Also, we can control the number of rats, roaches, and other disease carriers in our communities. We can also build immunity to disease by being vaccinated.

Still, there are diseases like AIDS that do not have a cure. We can only protect ourselves by avoiding these germs until scientists discover ways to prevent and cure them.

 Vocabulary

Find the words defined below in the scramble box.

a. high temperature
b. animal carrier of a disease-producing microbe (begins with "V")
c. drug from cinchona tree
d. very small organism
e. drug which fights microbes
f. to heal; make well

Just hitching a ride!

```
Q  U  I  N  I  N  E  R  C  M
S  F  E  V  E  R  R  L  M  R
H  T  B  E  U  C  S  R  E  Q
X  E  S  C  F  I  C  B  A  C
I  I  T  T  U  A  E  F  S  I
C  I  T  O  I  B  I  T  N  A
M  I  C  R  O  B  E  E  M  H
```

Ⓗ Weekly Lab

Where can microbes be found?

You need: 2 plastic bowls, unflavored gelatin, beef broth, cotton swabs, plastic wrap, marking pen

Step 1: Pick two areas you would like to test for microbes. Label each bowl.

Step 2: Make up a solution of unflavored gelatin. Use beef broth as the liquid. Pour 1/2 of this solution into each bowl. Allow the gelatin to solidify overnight.

Step 3: The next day, wipe each area with a cotton swab. Wipe one swab on the surface of the gelatin in Bowl 1. Wipe the other swab on the surface of the gelatin in Bowl 2. Cover each bowl with plastic wrap.

Step 4: Place the bowls together in one area. Check the bowls daily for signs of microbe growth.

In which areas of the school did you find the most microbes?
Why do you think this area had the most?
In which area of the school did you find the least growth?
Why do you think this area had the least?

![icon] Weekly Problem

Sneezes can travel through the air at a speed of 200 mph and carry as many as 100,000 microbes. The sneeze spreads out as it travels, so few of the microbes reach you.

If you were 1/2 mile away, how long would the sneeze take to reach you?
How long would it take a car traveling at 50 mph to reach you?

![icon] Writing for Science

Write a public health notice for the people of this town. What should they do to stop the spread of disease? Include at least 5 things. **Call a town meeting and plan an agenda.**
Who will speak? What demonstrations can you show?

⊟ Challenge

Write down the steps you used to find the answers to the Weekly Problem.
Compare with your classmates. Did everyone find the answer the same way?
Did anyone use the formula "distance equals rate times time" (D=RT)?
What is the easiest way to find the answers?

▦ Puzzle

Solve each problem. Write the letter from the box with the smallest number first. Continue writing letters from the boxes in increasing order. The answer is a word people used hundreds of years ago to describe eating without much appetite.

e 59 x 48		l 45 x 62
i 45 x 58		n 74 x 36
p 27 x 92		g 51 x 53

smallest ☐☐☐☐☐☐ largest

Bonus: Find out what the other two "old" words mean.

The Horse Returns to America

Can you imagine America without horses? That's what Columbus found when he arrived in 1492. A year later, his ships brought the modern horse to the Americas. But, he was actually returning the horse to its home.

The Earliest Horse

Scientists think that the family of horses began in North America about 55 million years ago. The earliest known horse was about the size of a dog. It had toes and a soft padded foot like a dog. It lived in the forest where the ground was soft. This little horse nibbled leaves and plants.

Over millions of years, the horse changed to **adapt** to different environments. As the land changed from forest to grassland, the horse's outer toes gradually disappeared and the middle toe **evolved** into a horny hoof. This made it possible for the horse to gallop on the harder ground. As the vegetation changed, the horse's teeth became larger and more square. The **muzzle** got longer in order to hold them. Gradually, the bodies of the horses became larger. The back became straighter and the legs got longer.

The Modern Horse

The modern horse traces its roots back to an animal that lived in the Western Hemisphere 5 million years ago. This animal **migrated** to Europe, Asia, and Africa where it continued to evolve. For some unknown reason, the horse disappeared from the Americas 10,000 years ago. However, it lived on in other parts of the world. About 6,000 years ago, the horse was tamed. It was used to pull war chariots, carriages, and plows. Eventually, people discovered they could ride horses, too.

When the Spanish brought the modern horse to America, it thrived and the herds multiplied. The Spanish soldiers used the horse in conquering the natives. Some natives thought the mounted warriors were a single creature. They were amazed by them. When they saw how valuable the horse was to the Spanish, they wanted their own. It was a long time before the natives got their own horses. When they did, the horse changed their lives forever.

33

⟨icon⟩ Vocabulary

Match the word with the part of the horse.
Use a dictionary or an encyclopedia to check your answers.

elbow

mane

forelock

knee

barrel

fetlock

withers

jowl

throttle

⟨M icon⟩ Weekly Lab

How can you determine the relative age of fossils?

You need:	four sheets of different colored clay (about .5 cm thick), 3 different kinds of cake decoration sprinkles, paper, pencil, a rock, table knife, 2 pieces of 5 cm x 10 cm cardboard

Step 1: Sprinkle one kind of cake decoration sprinkles ("fossils") thickly over a layer of clay. Cover it with another layer of clay. Repeat until all the clay layers are used.

Step 2: Cut the clay in half. Put one half on a piece of cardboard.

Step 3: Place the rock in the center of the other piece of cardboard. Drape the other half of the clay over it. Leave the rock showing. Push the clay gently so it molds to the rock.

Step 4: Use the knife to make a vertical cut in the center of each clay half.

Step 5: Make a drawing of where you find each type of "fossil" along the vertical cuts.

If the bottom layer of clay is the oldest, what does this tell you about the age of other fossils?
The rock represents the result of an earthquake.
How does an earthquake affect where you find the earliest fossils?

🐎 Weekly Problem

A horse's height is measured in hands. The earliest horse was about 3 hands high. The modern horse stands at 15 hands. **Give the height of both horses in millimeters, centimeters, and meters.**

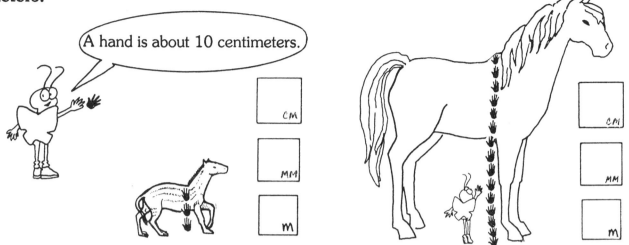

A hand is about 10 centimeters.

CM
MM
m

CM
MM
m

Bonus: Which of these would be best to measure with hands: length of a table, width of a pencil eraser, distance from school to home?
Make the measurement and compare with your friends.

📐 Writing for Science

Pretend you are a Native American. **Write a conversation between you and a friend about how the horse has changed your life.**

⊟ Challenge

Make a timeline in years that shows the evolution of the horse. Use the information on page 33 and these facts:

A. The original horse family is named Equidae.

B. Present day horses and their relatives belong to the genus Equus.

C. Equus spread across the world on land bridges.

D. The first horse to be tamed is Equus caballus.

▚ Puzzle

While on an expedition you find these fossilized footprints. **Write a paragraph interpreting them for your report.**

The Horse in America

Before Columbus brought the **horse** back to America, the natives did everything on foot. They had no animal large enough to ride or pull plows and wagons. After the horse came in 1493, it played an important role in the conquest and settlement of the Americas.

The Spanish and other explorers used the horse in battle. Their mobility on a horse gave them a great advantage and helped them to conquer the **Aztecs** and **Incas**. After their victories, the Spanish established large cattle **ranches** in Mexico. The horse played an important role on these ranches. From here, the horse spread rapidly to North America. By 1607, when the first towns were being settled in the East, there were already large cattle ranches and settlements in the West.

Native Americans and Horses

The Spanish knew how much power the horse gave them. They did not want the Native Americans to have horses. But the natives were able to get them by finding them or capturing them. By the end of the 1700s, every Native American group in the West had horses. Hunting tribes used them to chase buffalo on horse rather than on foot. Tribes that traveled could now own more possessions and let horses carry them from place to place. Some tribes developed a way of life based entirely on horses.

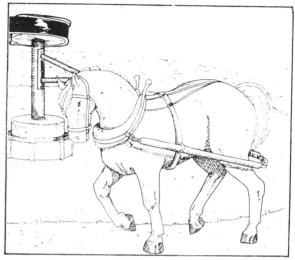

In the East, horses were important on the farms settled by the English. Horses also pulled wagons and carts in the towns. Horse-drawn carriages provided transportation between cities. Horses even powered machines in factories and businesses. One horse could provide enough power to run a small mill or a giant machine.

Westward Ho!

After the Civil War, many people formed horse-drawn wagon trains to go west and settle the frontier. They started farms and built fences around their land. This made the cattle ranchers angry since they wanted their huge herds to roam free to graze. Bitter fights broke out over fences.

When the railroad came, it was so important to the settlers that they called it the "Iron Horse." The railroad brought more settlers wanting land for farms. Horse soldiers came to fight the natives to make room for the newcomers. By the end of the century, the wide open plains were gone forever.

 Vocabulary

Write a sentence that shows you know the meaning of each expression.

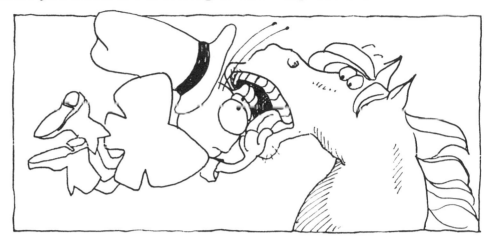

horsepower

horse sense

horse play

horse's mouth

riding herd

back in the saddle

Can you think of other "horse" expressions?

M Weekly Lab

How can a horse power a machine?

> **You need:** 3 tinkertoy wheels, 1 long tinkertoy rod,
> 3 short rods, large rubber band

Step 1: Put the end of the long rod into one of the wheels.

Step 2: Join the other 2 wheels and 2 of the short rods to alternate wheel-rod, wheel-rod.

Step 3: Push the last short rod into a side hole of the wheel that is in the center of the 2 short rods. This rod will be a lever.

Step 4: Hold both rods upright with the wheels at the top. Have your partner loop the rubber band around the wheels. Turn the lever.

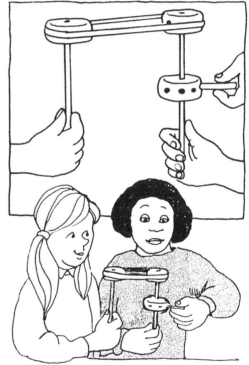

What happens to the rubber band and the other wheel?
If you hitched a horse to the lever, how could you use this motion to run a mill?
What other sources of energy could you use to turn the lever?

Weekly Problem

Horsepower is a term **coined** 200 years ago to compare the power of a steam engine to the power of work horses. A 1 hp engine is equal to 1.5 work horses. **Compute the number of horses replaced by each engine.**

4 hp   = —————— horses

10 hp   = —————— horses

7 hp   = —————— horses

30 hp   = —————— horses

Bonus: Find out the horsepower of your favorite car.
How many horses would it need if the engine didn't work?

Writing for Science

Pretend you live in Dodge City in 1875. Farmers want to build fences around their land and ranchers say no. You have to vote yes or no on this issue in 3 days. **Choose a side and write a list of arguments to support your decision.**

DISCOVERING SEEDS OF CHANGE

You need to buy horses for your ranch at a horse fair. You have $160 and have to spend it all. How many and what kinds of horses can you buy if you have to buy at least 1 carriage horse? What is the greatest number of horses you can get if you have to buy at least one cow pony? **Write a bill of sales for each purchase.**

Puzzle

Find each number. Then follow the directions to find out when the first rodeo was held.

The name of the trail south from Abilene, Texas has _____ letters.

The Pony Express operated for _____ months.

Barbed wire was patented in _____ .

The Golden Spike completed the railroad across America. It was driven on May _____, 1869.

Add the 3 smallest numbers and divide by 3. Subtract one.
Add this number to the biggest number.

Down on the Farm

America before Columbus did not have big **domesticated** animals like the horse, cow, pig, and sheep. In addition to the horse, Columbus brought these animals, along with goats and chickens, on his second voyage. They **thrived** in their new environment, and they multiplied rapidly. The Spanish brought more of their livestock to the mainland after they **conquered** the native people.

How Animals Changed America

The introduction of these animals changed the diet of the natives, their lives, and the land. People learned to **cultivate** the land to grow food for the animals. However, the large number of cattle destroyed the grasslands. What appeared to be an **inexhaustible** sea of grass before Columbus is today only a memory. We are not even sure what the grasslands looked like.

Farming and Ranching

As newcomers **colonized** America, they made many changes to the land. In the East, people set up farms with fences to keep their animals under control. In the West, cattle and horses were allowed to run free on large ranches. As farmers moved west, bitter fights broke out over fencing the land on the western Plains. Eventually, ranchers realized that growing corn and hay feed for the cattle would make them much fatter for market. So ranchers, too, fenced the land to keep their herds where they could control the food.

Advances in technology helped increase the **productivity** of farms. The invention of the plow enabled corn to be grown in massive amounts for cattle feed. The grasslands were plowed under to grow more food, and the number of cattle multiplied again. Corn, the horse, and cattle helped to create the world's largest livestock industry. However, it was out of harmony with the environment.

Conserving Our Land

When Columbus landed, no one worried about damaging the land. There was plenty of land, and the animals and people were few. People did not pay much attention to **conserving** the land. Farmers learned an important lesson in the 1930s when a long **drought** turned the overused land in Oklahoma into dust. The soil blew away with the wind. Today, ranchers and farmers practice **land management** to prevent overuse. Taking care with our natural resources will help protect our farm land.

Vocabulary

Use a thesaurus to find synonyms for these words from page 41:

Synonyms

domesticated   _____

thrived   _____

conquered   _____

cultivate   _____

inexhaustible   _____

colonized   _____

Weekly Lab

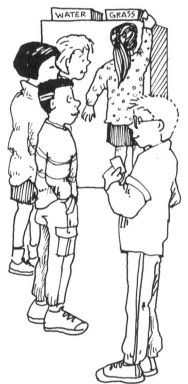

Teacher assistance needed.

You need: red, green, and blue construction paper, scissors, 2 boxes

Step 1: Cut the construction paper into equal numbers of pieces, each 3 centimeters square. Green represents grass and blue represents water. Put the blue and green squares into separate boxes.

Step 2: Mix red (danger) squares into each box. Put the boxes above eye level.

Step 3: Choose 2 groups of 5 students each. The Group 1 will be all horses, and the Group 2 will be 3 horses and 2 cows.

Step 4: Have each horse in Group 1 pick one square from each box. If a student picks a red square, that student puts the square back in the box and loses a turn. Keep picking squares in turns until they run out.

Step 5: Put the squares back into their boxes. Repeat step 3 with the second group. Have each horse pick one square and each cow choose 2 squares from each box.

How many turns can the Group 1 take?

How many horses go hungry and thirsty?

How many turns does Group 2 take?

What difference do the cows make to the food supply?

What happens when there is danger and no food and water?

☯ Weekly Problem

Lisa wants to buy some land for her goats. One piece of land is for sale and measures 60 meters by 121 meters. If she places a fence around the land how many yards of fencing will she need?

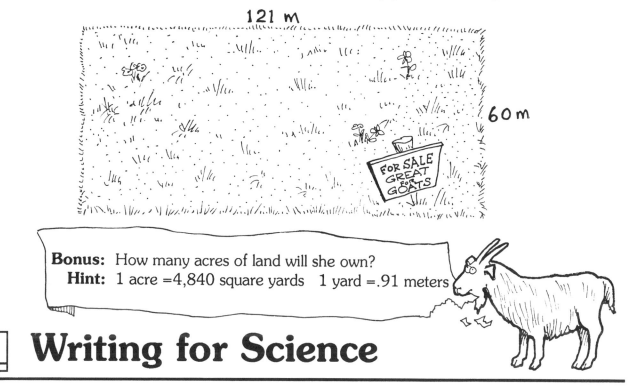

121 m

60 m

FOR SALE GREAT for GOATS

Bonus: How many acres of land will she own?
Hint: 1 acre = 4,840 square yards   1 yard = .91 meters

⛺ Writing for Science

Write a 3 minute news report to summarize what is happening on farms today.
How do farms operate? What do they grow? What new technology do farmers have?

FARM FACTS

NEWS and VIEWS

⊡ Challenge

Amber asked 12 of her friends what they thought caused them the most stress while they were working on the Down on the Farm project. The circle graph shows the results of the poll. **Use the graph to answer the questions below.**

1. Which activity caused the most stress?
2. Which activity caused stress for 3 students?
3. Name 2 activities that caused stress for a total of 4 students.
4. Name a combination of activities that caused stress for half of the students.

▦ Puzzle

If 3 hens lay 3 eggs in 3 days, how many eggs can 300 hens lay in 300 days?
(Hint: Find out how long it takes 1 hen to lay 1 egg.)

Archaeology

Would you be excited to find stone **ruins**? Well, **archaeologists are**. For over 10 years, archaeologists have been studying the ruins of **Galways Plantation** on the Caribbean island of Montserrat. They found a **windmill** once used for crushing **sugar cane**, and a **boiling house** used for extracting sugar from the crushed cane.

Sugar in the Caribbean

Who lived on this **plantation** long ago? History tells us that English **colonists** and their **indentured** Irish **servants** first settled the island in 1632. Over a century earlier, Columbus brought sugarcane to the Caribbean. It thrived wherever it was planted. But it also changed the land forever. Two-thirds of the island's **rain forest** was cut to make large sugar plantations.

Plantations needed many workers to raise the sugarcane under the hot tropical sun. It was their main cash crop. To make the sugar trade as profitable as possible, plantation owners wanted workers they did not have to pay. They exchanged sugar for **enslaved Africans**. Plantations grew and more sugar was shipped to satisfy Europe's sweet tooth.

Discovering the Past

Digging up the past is what archaeology is all about. The process of digging for objects is called **excavating**. First, archaeologists draw maps by walking over the area and taking aerial photographs. Then, they carefully excavate the dirt, sift it, and find **artifacts** used by those who once lived in the area. An artifact is a tool or object used by people of long ago. To understand what the Galways Plantation artifacts mean, they study old books and interview people whose families have been on the island many generations. Archaeologists have been able to put together a picture of life on this plantation.

Clues in the Slave Village

Slave living quarters were made of wood with a roof of palm leaves. None of the original buildings are standing today. But excavated bits of bone, pieces of pottery, coins, **slate pencils**, **metal graters**, and a **stone griddle** provide clues about the slaves' daily life.

Rather than rest during their breaks, slaves grew food in secret gardens, made crafts, and tended their own livestock. They made flat disks of **cassava bread** by grating cassava and baking it on griddles. At Sunday market they sold or traded these goods for things from Europe and China or from local farms. Plantation owners even bought food at the market. Slaves regarded market days as a right and resisted attempts to regulate it. Despite the hardships of the plantation, the enslaved people were able to create a community of their own.

⊞ Weekly Lab

Purpose: to develop and apply a classification system for artifacts from an archaeological dig.

Materials: large 'dig' box from teacher, trowel, brushes, sieve, pencil, paper, marking pen, spoons, measuring stick, newspaper, string, tape

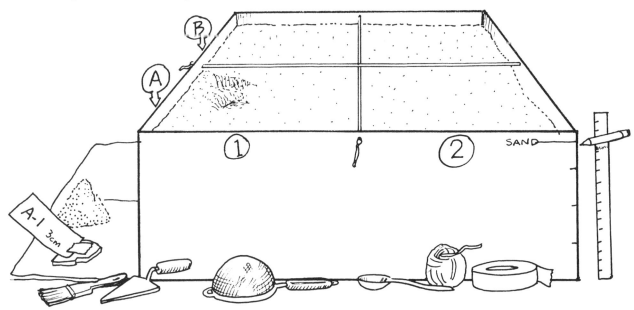

1. Develop a code and data sheet to record sorted artifacts by type, depth, and grid section.

2. Mark level of sand with pen.

3. Divide box opening with a 2x2 grid of string.

4. Attempt to guess what artifacts you might find.

5. Dig for artifacts in top 10 cm of sand. Brush them clean.

6. Sort and label artifacts.

7. Measure an artifact and draw it.

8. Record all data on the classification sheet.

9. Continue with each 10 cm of sand.

Write your results in Writing for Science.

Weekly Problem

Here are census figures for Montserrat in the years 1678 and 1729.
Answer the questions based on the data.

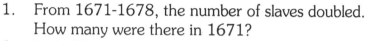

Population of Montserrat			
Year	1671	1678	1729
Africans		1000	5000
English/Irish		3000	1100

1. From 1671-1678, the number of slaves doubled. How many were there in 1671?
2. In 1729, there were 5000 Africans. What is the percentage increase after 1678?
3. In 1729, there were 1100 English/Irish. What is the percentage decrease after 1678?
4. Why do you think the number of Africans increased during this period while the number of English/Irish decreased?

 # Writing for Science

Use the scientific way of writing up your Weekly Lab results.

Step 1: Write your hypothesis. What artifacts did you guess you would find?
Step 2: Write down your materials and procedure. What did you do? What materials did you use? What did you use them to do?
Step 3: Write down your results. What did you discover while doing the experiment? Use your data classification sheet to help you organize your results.
Step 4: Write your conclusion about your dig.

The following questions will help you with your conclusion.

1. Why is it important to sort and label each artifact?
2. Why is it important to record the depth of your artifact?
3. Were all the objects you found really artifacts?
4. Did you have to revise your classification sheet?
5. Was there anything you would do differently if you did the dig again?

■ Challenge

Pretend you are an archaeologist excavating a site the shape of a rectangle. The length of the site is 80 meters, and the width is 50 meters. A tree is growing in an area 20 meters by 20 meters within the site.

How many square meters must you excavate if you do not use the area around the tree?

Here is what you will need to know before beginning:

1. the formula for finding the area of a rectangle
2. the area of the site
3. the area of the tree's location

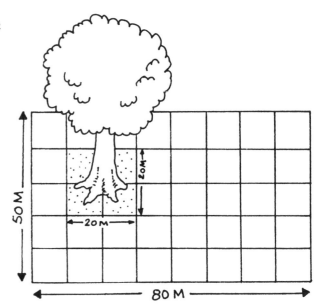

■ Puzzle

Use the clues to complete the puzzle.
Hint: All the answers are computer words.

Across

1. to transfer information from a disk to a computer's memory
3. a list of instructions to the computer
7. an error in the program
8. a computer screen
9. a flashing marker

Down

1. part of a computer program that is done over and over
2. what makes a robot work
4. word that makes the computer execute a program
5. list of choices on the screen
6. to start up a computer

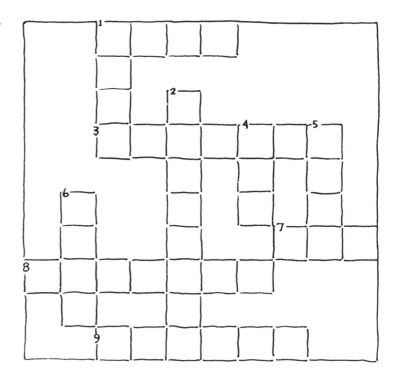

Sugar

Sugar was first used in the Far East about 2,000 years ago. Europeans discovered sugar in the Middle Ages when **merchants** brought it from the **Middle East.** Only rich people could afford it because it costs 70 times more than it does today.

When Did Sugar Arrive in the Americas?

In the late 15th century Christopher Columbus brought the **sugar cane** plant to the **West Indies.** The hot **tropical climate** was ideal for its growth and farms called **plantations** were established. With Africans imported to do the work for little or no wages, plantation owners soon became rich. It wasn't long before sugar became know as "white gold" in Europe.

Where Does Sugar Come From?

Two plants, the sugar cane and the sugar beet, supply most of the sugar we consume. The sugar cane is a tall grass that grows best in a hot, moist climate. The sugar beet is a root vegetable that is suited to **temperate** climate. Like all plants, they live by absorbing water through their roots, and carbon dioxide and sunlight through their leaves. During this process, known as **photosynthesis,** all these factors combine to form a type of sugar. This sugar supplies the sugar cane and sugar beet with energy.

Since the early 1900s, people in the United States have increased their sugar consumption. We now get more calories from sugar than we do from starch. Sugar is not a harmful substance but it is known to cause tooth decay in youths and adults who fail to brush and floss their teeth.

How to Reduce Sugar Intake

There are many ways to reduce the intake of **refined** sugar. People should eat more starches and natural sugars in the form of fruits, vegetables, and grain products. We should reduce our consumption of soft drinks and baked goods. We should avoid processed foods with lots of sugar. People can watch for words on food labels that list sugar as a primary ingredient. The body cannot distinguish between different kinds of sugar. It all reduces to sucrose, a primary source of energy for the body. Many scientists claim that it is not what kind of sugar you eat, it's the amount you eat.

Some of us may even be wearing sugar or its **by-products**. Sugar is sometimes used for treating cloth to make it crease-resistant. It is used in livestock feed, plastics, wallboard, nylon fiber, and many drugs and dyes. There is little waste in sugar production.

▣ Weekly Lab

Background: Sugar is found in all plants. It is a universal form of energy for living things. Many animals, insects, and humans seem to have a natural preference for things that are sweet.

Purpose: To observe the natural attraction of other life forms for sugar products.

Materials: 4 jar lids, water, honey, lemon, salt, bowl, spoon, masking tape

1. Label the jar lids 'salt', 'lemon', 'honey', and 'water'. Use masking tape.

2. Mix a solution of salt and water. Pour some of the solution into the lid labeled 'salt'.

3. Squeeze a lemon into the lid labeled 'lemon'.

4. Pour honey into the lid labeled 'honey'.

5. Pour plain water into the lid labeled 'water'.

6. Place the lids outside on the ground. Try to find a place where there are already insects, such as near an ant hill. Leave the lids in place for at least a day.

7. Observe which lids the insects prefer. Try to estimate how many insects go to each lid.

8. Repeat experiment adding an artificial sweetener to your test.

Questions:
1. Why do you think insects chose the lid that they did?
2. Does one lid contain a food item that could sustain life without forms of food?
3. Which sweeteners were more attractive to the insects?
4. Did it make any difference when you used artificial sweeteners?

![icon] Weekly Problem

You are starting your own business by baking a new type of cookie. The cookie dough requires three kilograms of sugar for each batch. Sugar costs $2.58 per kilogram. An artificial sweetener costs $4.33 per kilogram, but it is five times as sweet as the sugar. Which one is the better buy for your company?

![icon] Writing for Science

Write a dialogue between a sugar beet and sugar cane. Discuss the similarities and differences.

⊞ Challenge

The map below shows producers of sugar cane and sugar beets. **Explain how the climate affects each industry. Make a bar graph showing the countries with the largest sugar cane production. Make another bar graph showing the countries with the largest sugar beet production.**

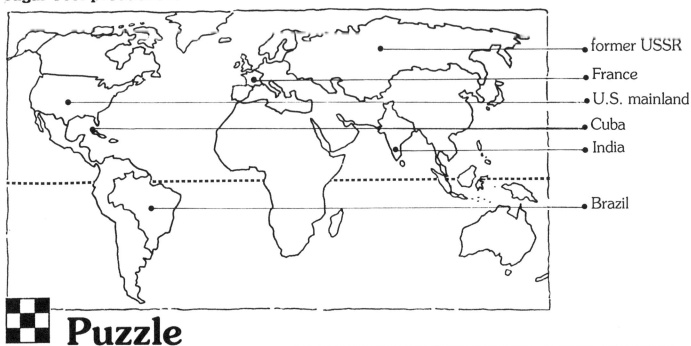

former USSR
France
U.S. mainland
Cuba
India
Brazil

▦ Puzzle

The top 10 United States sugar-producing states are hidden in the word find below. **Locate each state on the map. Decide if each state grows sugar cane or sugar beets.**

```
M A D I R O L F T H I A
A I W H N H S X E M D T
N O R P S A X E T I A O
T B E N C D G B R N P S
X C L O U I S I A N A E
A K S A R B E N H O N N
A I N R O F I L A C K N
O F I L A C H A W A I I
A T O K A D H T R O N M
```

SUGAR
CANE
BEET

CORN   POTATO   DISEASE   HORSE   SUGAR

Technology

A Changing World

Technology is the application of science. **Technologists** and **technicians** take the research results of our engineers and scientists and convert them into applications that improve the quality of human life. Technology has changed the way we think and communicate with each other. Your grandparents probably did not have the convenience of television and telephones. Today, we can talk to anyone in the world in a matter of seconds. We are able to interact with different cultures and people from our living rooms.

Christopher Columbus had no means to communicate with Spain and Italy once he was at sea. He didn't have the benefit of **sonar radar**, satellites, morris codes, and computers to aid his voyages and sea explorations. He had to rely on his personal skills, **manual** records and journals, and his developed instincts and sea experience. Communication at sea with the outside world was non existent.

A Closer World

The Walt Disney Song, "It's a Small World" reminds us that we can communicate with other countries very easily. We know that the size of the earth has not changed. Measured at sea level, the diameter of the earth around the equator is 12,756.8 kilometers. However, the ways in which we use technology has brought us closer together.

Modern Technology

Sophisticated methods of communication have interlinked the parts of the world and have given us the possibility of unlimited benefit. Scientists have been able to advance their research, and by the use of technology, advance health care and medicine. Because of modern technology, people can live healthier and longer lives. In a few years, maybe months, technology will help scientists find cures for cancer, aids, and other health problems that threaten human life. Just suppose Columbus had only one of our modern communication devices. Think of how different his voyages would have been!

⬛ Weekly Lab

What materials make the best walkie talkie?

Purpose: to determine which types of materials carry sound better

Materials: paper cups, styrofoam cups, tin cans, string, thin copper wire, picture hanging wire

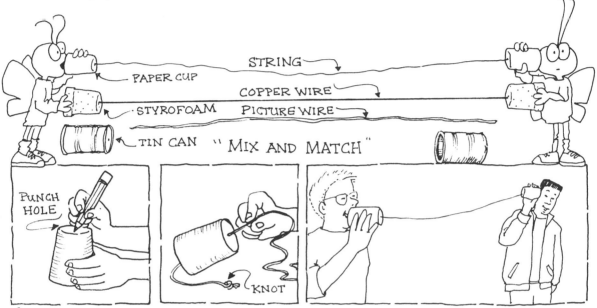

STRING
PAPER CUP
COPPER WIRE
STYROFOAM
PICTURE WIRE
TIN CAN   "MIX AND MATCH"
PUNCH HOLE
KNOT

Procedures:

1. Look at the **picture diagram** to determine how to put your walkie talkie together.

2. First, use paper cups and string.

3. Write down what you discovered or learned.

4. Second, use styrofoam cups and thin copper wire.

5. Write down your results.

6. Change materials, make other **communicators**, and write down your results.

7. Continue this **process** until you have made as many communicators as you can.

8. Write down your results for each.

9. When you complete your experiments and have tried all of your walkie talkies, go to **Writing for Science**

Weekly Problem

Today, with modern technology, you can have lunch in New York City and dinner in London on the same day. Suppose you were traveling to London on the supersonic airliner at 1350 kilometers per hour and your trip took 3 hours.

1.   How many kilometers was your trip?
2.   Suppose your friend left at the same time on a jet traveling at 675 kilometers per hour. How many additional hours would it take him to reach London?
3.   How many miles would you travel round trip?   **Hint:** .621 miles = 1 kilometer

Writing for Science

Write the results of your Weekly Lab using the Scientific method. Use the following procedure.

1.   Write your original assumption.
2.   Write your procedure. Tell what you did to put your walkie talkies together and to make them work.
3.   Write your **results**. What happened? The following questions may help you.
     a.   Which types of ear/speaker phones worked best?
     b.   Which type of connection worked best?
     c.   Did the length of your connections make any difference?
4.   Write your conclusions. What did you learn?
     a.   Describe your best communication device.
     b.   What would be very important information to tell your friend if she was going to make a walkie talkie?

Challenge

Technology has helped **NASA** advance its space shuttle transportation system. The system has four components: two solid rocket boosters (SRB's); one external tank (ET); and the orbiter.

1. Fueled SRB's weigh 586 metric tons each. If each SRB burns off 4 metric tons of fuel per second during lift-off, how much fuel has been consumed after 2 minutes?

2. At this point, approximately how much does an SRB weigh?

Puzzle

Across
1. sounds your heart make
4. to spring off the ground
7. a period of time in history
8. put in motion
9. carry out or perform
13. people trained in sports
14. he won a medal in the _____ -put
16. having to do with sight

Down
1. the sun and moon are heavenly
2. rhymes with farm
3. you can do this with money
5. won at the Olympics
6. short for professional
10. strength and staying power
11. to inquire about
12. I _____ you
15. note on the scale after "la"

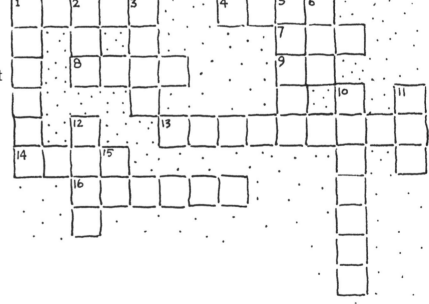

The Environment and You

How often have you heard the question: Do you believe that you can make a difference? Columbus had no idea that his voyages would begin a major exchange of information and resources that would make a difference in our **environment** and **lifestyles** 500 years later.

Today we realize that our planet is not **infinite** but rather **finite**. We know that we have only one world and one environment. We must work together to preserve our valuable resources. What can we do? There are many things an individual can do.

First, we must educate ourselves about environmental issues and then, most importantly, act upon what we learn. For example, we can **recycle** and reduce waste.

Second, we must make wise choices about environmental issues if necessary. For example, each year millions of acres of tropical rainforests are burned to make way for agriculture. Yet, rainforest plants are used in making many medicines sold today. Although there is much we do not yet know about the rainforest, we do know that we need to safeguard the plants and animals that can live only in this very **unique biome**.

Finally, we need to consider changing our lifestyle in order to help save our **fragile** planet. The growing population of the earth is placing more and more demand upon the environment. Humans have expected and taken so much from the earth that water and air pollution threaten our very existence. The earth's ozone layer is also being depleted daily.

Our planet is like a spider web. It is interconnected. What each one of us does has an impact on someone somewhere. We must learn to appreciate our valuable resources, to care about others, and to plan for our future. We must continue to exchange information and use our technological advances to protect our **endangered** planet.

![] Weekly Lab

Purpose: to examine the decomposition of waste

Materials: 2 aquariums, coarse gravel, dirt, notebook paper, plastic wrap, tape, water, observation chart

Waste materials to be tested: lettuce, plastic spoon, aluminum foil, paper

Procedure:
1. Form a hypothesis. State the order in which the waste material will decompose: first, second, third, and fourth.
2. Prepare both aquariums by placing 5 cm of gravel on the bottom. Cover gravel with 20—25 cm of dry soil.
3. In each aquarium, bury a piece of lettuce, of paper, of foil, and a plastic spoon.
4. Cover the top of one aquarium with plastic wrap and seal with tape.
5. Sprinkle one cup of water in the uncovered aquarium.
6. Place both aquariums in the same location.
7. Dig up objects weekly and make observations. Rebury objects and keep the uncovered aquarium moist by adding water when necessary.

Make an observation chart like the one below and record your data.

Date	Lettuce	Plastic Spoon	Aluminum Foil	Paper

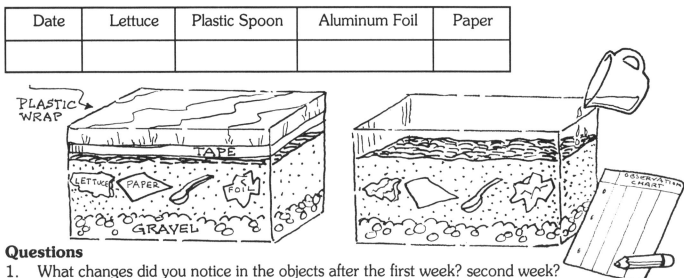

Questions
1. What changes did you notice in the objects after the first week? second week?
2. Which materials began to decompose first? Why?
3. What differences in decomposition did you notice between the two aquariums? Why?
4. What does this tell you about materials at a landfill?
5. What actions could you take to decrease the volume of refuse that presently goes into our landfills?
6. Why is waste management important?
7. Log all your data and observations. Then go to **Writing for Science**.

Weekly Problem

Acid rain is the waste that comes from pollution in the **atmosphere**. **Use the pH scale below to answer the questions.**

1. What is the pH of "normal rain"?
2. What is the pH of the lowest rain measured? Where was this rain measured?
3. Which lake water has less acid: the Great Lakes or the Adirondack Lakes?
4. At what pH are all fish dead?
5. What is the difference between the pH of the water in the Great Lakes and the lowest rain pH measured?

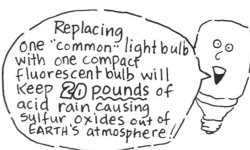

Replacing one "common" light bulb with one compact fluorescent bulb will keep **20** pounds of acid rain causing sulfur oxides out of EARTH'S atmosphere!!

 # Writing for Science

Use the data you recorded in the Weekly Lab to write your results.

Procedures
1. State your hypothesis.
2. What was your experiment? (Write out the procedures you followed.)
3. What did you observe after each week of your experiment?
4. What did you conclude? Was your hypothesis correct?
5. Explain why your results were different from your hypothesis.
6. If your hypothesis was correct, what did you learn from your experiment?

Remember the 3 R's
Reduce
Reuse
Recycle!

⊔ Challenge

The average person in the United States throws away 4 pounds of garbage each day. The average 4-door compact car weighes approximately one ton. It costs about $30 to dispose of each ton of **refuse**. Using these **statistics**, make a bar graph to compare how many tons of garbage are disposed of by:

1. your school
2. all the schools in your community
3. all the people in your community

Bonus: What percent of the nation's garbage does your state dispose?

▣ Puzzle

Some Earth resources are renewable, and some are not. Some materials are nonrenewable because they are the result of **geological** processes that take million of years to complete. Once they are used up, they are gone forever. **Use the library to complete the following.**

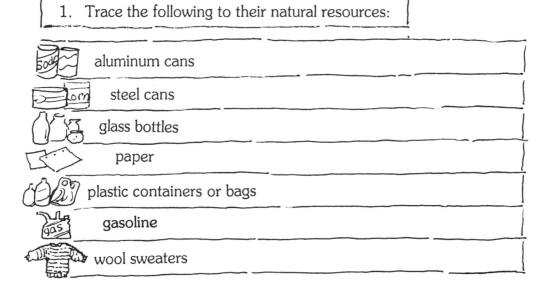

1. Trace the following to their natural resources:

aluminum cans

steel cans

glass bottles

paper

plastic containers or bags

gasoline

wool sweaters

2. Determine which containers or materials came from a nonrenewable source.

Teaching Notes

Sailing the Ocean Blue

BACKGROUND

Christopher Columbus did not discover America. There were already advanced civilizations in the Americas long before Columbus's voyage. Columbus is generally accepted to be the first European to encounter the Americas and return information on what he saw. His voyage opened a great age of discovery. Worldwide trade followed and the two worlds exchanged the seeds of change. Corn and the potato went to Europe and the horse came back to America.

Columbus was born in Italy and wanted to become a sailor at an early age. He studied the books made available to him by the invention of the printing press. By studying geography, he thought he had found a shorter route to the Indies. He would sail west across the Atlantic Ocean. However, no one would give him money to support this venture. Finally, King Ferdinand and Queen Isabella of Spain agreed to finance the voyage.

The Voyage Begins
In August, 1492, Columbus sailed with a crew of 90 men and 3 ships, the Santa Maria, the Pinta, and the Nina. His ships were tiny. The largest, the Santa Maria, was only 90 feet long. It carried a crew of 40 men. Conditions aboard the ships were primitive. Sailors bailed out seawater with buckets. There was no refrigeration, so food spoiled readily. Even though pumps worked constantly to remove bilge water, there was always a smell. Mutiny was a persistent threat to Columbus.

Even though the conditions were primitive and the ships lacked many instruments we now take for granted, Columbus was sailing with the finest ships and equipment of his time. He took advantage of the many recent advances in sailing to take the first voyage into the uncharted waters that lay to the west.

The Importance of Science
There were great improvements in ship construction during the 15th century. Improved masts, square sails, and larger hulls all helped make long ocean voyages possible.

The invention of the printing press made maps and charts available. There were also many scientific instruments invented by this time. Columbus had the compass to show directions. He also had the quadrant to find the ship's position from the sun or stars. However, these instruments could not always be used in rough waters. Columbus often relied on the method of dead reckoning. This is a combination of estimating the ship's position and speed, plus using the navigator's knowledge of the sea.

During the voyage Columbus had ordered the ships to steer due west. One day he noticed the compass's magnetic needle moving toward the northwest. By observing the position of the North Star, he realized that geographical north does not coincide with magnetic north. This discovery of magnetic variation was another example of Columbus's superb navigational skills.

The Log
On October 11, 1492, the cannon was fired as a sign that land had been sighted. Columbus and his crew landed on a small island the next day. He thought he was in India, but he had reached the Americas. He named the island San Salvador. For the next few weeks, his ships explored the islands, traded with the natives, and made the necessary repairs.

On Christmas Eve, the Santa Maria wrecked and only two ships would return to Spain. Columbus left a colony of 39 men behind. He hoped they could convert the natives to Christianity. When he returned on his second voyage, they were all dead.

He would make a total of four voyages to the "West Indies" and would see people settle in this area. He did not prove to be a very good administrator in the settlements and he was sent back in chains on his last voyage. He died, broken-hearted, in 1506.

Misconception: Many people think that Columbus sailed west to prove the earth was round. In truth, most educated people already knew this. Columbus was looking for a shorter route to the Indies.

ACTIVITIES

Main Concept: Better ships and scientific instruments

made Columbus's voyages possible. Columbus was an excellent navigator and scientist.

Vocabulary
Columbus sailed for the king and queen of Spain.

Answers: 1. c, 2. d, 3. b, 4. e, 5. f, 6. a, 7. h, 8. g

Tell students to ask a Spanish-speaking friend for help, or use a Spanish dictionary if they have trouble guessing the matches.

Weekly Lab
Use a flagpole, tree, or tall building. To save protractors, students could copy the protractor onto a piece of cardboard and cut it out. Be sure the students stand on the same level as the tall object.

Weekly Problem
You may have to help the students with the angle construction. Put the line of the protractor over the line FL (with some protractors this line is different from the edge or bottom). Make a mark next to the number of the measured angle. Draw a line from that mark to point F. Do the same thing to construct the right angle at L (or use a square piece of cardboard). Their final measurement (in centimeters) will be line YW. Multiplying that number by 100 will give the height of the object. Let students compare answers.

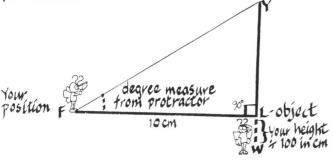

Challenge
Students may need help using the map scale.

Puzzle
Some words include navigate, navigator, naval, nautical, navy, navigable, and navigation. Use the dictionary to find other words.

A-Maizing Corn

BACKGROUND

"Then in the spring when she is replete
with living waters
All different kings of corn
In our earth mother
We shall lay to rest."
(from the Zuni ritual poem, "Prayer of the Firekeeper at the Winter Solstice")

At the time of Columbus's arrival, corn was the most widely grown plant in the Americas and the most important food of Native Americans. But corn as we know it (domesticated corn) cannot survive in the wild. The seeds, or kernels, are so firmly attached to the cob that they do not disperse easily. How did corn become such an important food?

It is generally accepted that corn was first grown in Mesoamerica. This is the area which encompasses most of present day Mexico and parts of Guatemala and Honduras. Archaeologists have found tiny corn cobs in Mexican deposits that are over 7,000 years old.

Corn Makes Settlement Possible
Initially, the ancient Mesoamericans were hunters and gatherers. Somehow they learned to plant the seeds of the wild grasses they gathered. One of these wild grasses, *teosinte*, is thought by many scientists to be the ancestor of domesticated corn. Perhaps the people learned to choose the biggest and best seeds for planting. In this way, over the course of many hundreds of years, they could play an active role in the development of corn. As the food supply became more stable, people began to settle in villages near their fields. Because of the abundance of food, some villagers could devote time to other activities, like weaving, sculpting, and studying the stars. Eventually large and prosperous cities grew and dominated entire regions.

Corn Travels to Different Environments
Corn spread from Mesoamerica to the south and north as Native Americans successfully developed plants and planting methods suitable for the local environments. People in swampy areas cut water vegetation, piled it high, and covered it with mud to make garden plots. At the other extreme were tribes in the desert areas of present-day southwest United States who built irrigation systems. The Hopi tribe developed a low-growing corn plant that used water efficiently and put most of its energy into the cob. By the time Columbus arrived there were hundreds of varieties of corn growing all over North and South America.

Uses of Corn
Perhaps the oldest method of cooking corn was to pop it! Archaeologists have found kernels of popcorn, both popped and unpopped, at some ancient sites. Corn was dried, stacked by color and stored for later use, sometimes in underground storage vaults. One method for softening the kernels was to soak them in water and wood ashes. They could then be ground for use in breads, gruels, and beverages. Dried kernels were also used as beads and game markers.

Other parts of the corn plant were used as well. The sweet, hollow stalk could be chewed like candy or used as a medicine container. Leaves were used as bandages and silks were used to make medicine. The husks were woven into mats and baskets and even moccasins. Nothing was wasted!

Corn as Part of Native American Spiritual Lives

Because the very survival of Native Americans was so dependent on corn, corn became an integral part of their spiritual lives. A perfect ear of corn was tucked in with a new baby so he or she would have good health and good luck. Elaborate ceremonies and myths developed, centered especially around planting and harvesting. Sacred cornmeal was sprinkled on newly planted fields and the first ear harvested was shared with the Corn Spirit. Offerings, even human sacrifices, were made to ensure that the Corn Spirit was pleased. In dry regions, rituals during the growing season centered on the Rain God. Some of these rituals are still performed today. Native Americans called corn "our life, that which sustains us." It is this gift that they have given to the rest of the world.

Storytelling/Writing for Science

A myth is a traditional story of unknown authorship. It is used to explain some phenomenon of nature or the customs or religious rites of a people. The following is an adaptation of a Pueblo myth which explains the origin of corn and its many colors. Be dramatic as you tell this myth to your class!

Pueblo Myth of the Corn Maidens

In the beginning there was no corn—only grass. So the first people prayed to the Sun to send them more to eat. They built a fire in honor of the Sun and offered him the most colorful grass seeds. The Sun, in return, sent six sisters from the Seed People. They were the beautiful Corn Maidens.

The Corn Maidens were dressed in white capes that were decorated with all the colors of the rainbow. They danced through the grasses by the light of the fire and, as they danced, the grasses grew tall with long leaves and feathery tassels.

As the Corn Maidens touched one of the plants, the fire burned bright yellow. They touched another and the fire glowed red. Then they touched a third and the fire sent up clouds of blue smoke. As they touched the fourth the fire burned hot and white. And when they touched the fifth plant, sparks of many colors went up into the sky. Finally they touched the sixth plant, and the fire died down and left only black ashes. The six colors of corn known to the Pueblos, yellow, red, blue, white, speckle, and black, thus came to be.

ACTIVITIES

Main Concept: Corn was first grown by Native Americans long before Columbus came. Besides being a very important food, corn was used in a variety of ways. The Native Americans used all parts of the plant. Nothing was wasted. There were many ceremonies that centered on the importance of corn. Native Americans discovered ways to make the corn bigger and better.

Vocabulary

Answers: 1. prehistoric, 2. preexisting, 3. prefabricated, 4. pre-Columbian. Use the dictionary to find other words that begin with "pre." Challenge students to think of a certain number of words, or see who can think of the most.

Weekly Lab

You will need medium-sized rocks for this lab. Watch the children as they grind the corn. Caution them not to eat the ground corn (there may be pieces of rock in it). Have the students time the soaking so all the cups are ready at the same time. (Add water to cup 1 the night before the lab, cup 2 one hour before the lab, and cup 3 five minutes before the lab.)

Weekly Problem

Answers: 1. ⊥ 2. ⊥ 3. . . . . Bonus: 22

Writing for Science

A myth is a story that uses fiction to explain a fact. The ancient Mesoamericans sometimes drew a codex to illustrate a myth. Before class, read the myth of the Corn Maidens. Then tell (or have a student tell), not read, the myth to the class. Have the students work in small groups to create myths of their own. The members of each group should share in the task of illustrating their myth. Then have them connect the sections of their codex to make one long codex to share with the rest of the class.

Challenge

Make sure students know what an archaeologist is (a scientist who excavates, or digs, to find out about people who lived long ago). Students can work in groups and then share their work with the class.

Normally you would expect plant material to decompose in a relatively short amount of time. The dry climate in New Mexico prevented deterioration of the corn in the cave. The oldest cobs (from the deepest layers) were small. Successively smaller cobs were found in successively deeper layers. This shows that the people who grew corn here were able to develop, over the course of several thousand years, bigger and better varieties of corn.

They also knew how to pop corn. You might also find other items from the daily lives of these people: tools, pottery, perhaps ceremonial items.

Puzzle

Answers: (15, 12, 1, 15) (8, 12, 19, 4, 12) (6, 14, 6, 15, 1, 19, 17, 6) (14, 6) "That which sustains us."

Growing Corn

BACKGROUND

Corn has played an important role from the earliest days of the settlement of North America. In 1620 William Bradford wrote of the Pilgrims' arrival at Plymouth:

"They had no friends to welcome them, nor inns to entertain and refresh their weather beaten bodies, nor houses—much less towns to repair to . . . What could they see but a desolate wilderness full of wild beasts and wild men?"

Yet these "wild men" saved the Pilgrims from starvation by teaching them which plants to eat, particularly corn. Even earlier, in 1607 at Jamestown, Captain John Smith staved off starvation by obtaining corn seeds from local tribes. By 1630 the Virginia colony was exporting excess corn. In Colonial America, corn was so valuable that it was sometimes used as money.

Indeed, corn became a valuable gift from the Native Americans to both the settlers and the people of Europe. Crews of sailing ships took seeds and plants from the Americas to Europe. Although corn was reluctantly accepted at first, by the 18th century it had become one of the world's major food crops. Today, corn is grown worldwide, with the greatest production in the Corn Belt of the United States. The 1990 U.S. crop was estimated at 7.9 billion bushels worth over $18 billion.

Planting Techniques
Native American farmers sowed corn seeds in small fields (*milpa*) or in mounds, pushing soil into hills to support growing stalks. "Hilling" also minimized soil erosion. Beans and squash were planted around corn. Squash leaves kept soil shaded, preserving moisture and preventing weeds. The cornstalks served as bean poles, and beans added nitrogen to the soil. Without nitrogen, corn leaves turn light yellow-green, and the stalks are spindly and stunted.

Before chemical fertilizers, farmers often adopted the Native American practice of rotating corn with beans. Today, innovations in planting and harvesting, chemical fertilizers, weed and pest control, and hybrid seeds have increased yield to over 100 bushels per acre. Farmers can now produce 150 bushels in the time it took an early settler to produce one.

What Is Corn?
Corn, or maize, is a member of the grass family. It must be planted annually. Cultivated corn is dependent on human help for survival. Corn husks do not open by themselves. Humans must remove the dried seeds and plant them. Cornstalks are topped with a tassel (male flower) full of pollen. Silks (female flower) hang from the end of each ear. Pollen travels down each silk to the cob. Thus fertilized, a baby plant forms within each seed (kernel).

Photosynthesis
Unlike humans, plants make their own food for growth. Leaves draw carbon dioxide from the air and water from the soil. In the presence of sunlight, these raw materials are converted into sugar. Sugar molecules join and are stored as starch. Corn plants store starch around each fertilized seed. This stored starchy food is what we eat.

When a seed is planted, this starch nourishes the baby plant until it sprouts.

Biodiversity
To reproduce true to type, corn must not be near the pollen of another variety of corn. For example, to produce sweet Silver Queen corn, its silks must be pollinated by Silver Queen pollen. Cross-pollinating with another of the 650 varieties of sweet corn will produce different characteristics. Hybrid corn results from crossbreeding inbred lines and careful selection of seeds for desired characteristics. Despite high yields from hybrid corn, it is important to save diverse corn seeds to enable us to develop different varieties that will grow in new areas, that will resist plant diseases or insects, or that will produce higher quality protein.

ACTIVITIES

Main Concept: Each corn seed has food value as well as potential to grow. Native Americans conserved land space and used organic methods in farming. Diversity of seed stocks is necessary to match the climate and use of the corn.

Vocabulary
Answers: 1. verb, 2. noun, 3. noun, 4. verb, 5. verb, 6. noun

Let students work in teams to find other words (for example: uses, weeds, seed, rows, wind, sprinkles).

Weekly Lab
Ask students to make predictions. Place the cold temperature cups in a refrigerator. Extend the lab by putting a dot of indelible ink on the root as it emerges. Does the root grow at the seed or at the tip? (Tip.) Students could also compute the fraction or percent of seeds that germinated per condition, graph the number of seeds sprouting per day, or graph the length of the root each day.

If a refrigerator is not available, vary the amount of water per cup and monitor growth. Students could also design an experiment to test the effect of sunlight on corn plant growth. Have them continue their logs and share results with the class.

Weekly Problem
Review rules of rounding with students. These are rounded to the 100 millions place. Have students note that corn production is in millions of bushels.

Answers: 1. 1,400,000,000, 2. 200,000,000 or 200 million, 3. less, 4. 600,000,000 or 600 million

Have them use the rounded number for calculating.

Writing for Science
Extend this activity by having students do research on specific Native American tribes and their uses of corn.

Corn Today

BACKGROUND

Corn is America's gold! Just as it was for the people who preceded us in this hemisphere, corn is a basic food plant and more. Lots more! Corn is not only used as food and fodder, but, thanks to corn refining technology, it also is used to produce thousands of items we use every day.

  In the United States, more acres are planted with corn than with any other commodity. In fact, last year U.S. farmers harvested over 7.5 billion bushels.

Uses for Corn

What happens to all that corn? Some of the corn crop comes directly to our tables since Americans eat, on the average, over 7 pounds of sweet corn per year. The bulk of the crop, however, is field corn. A large percentage of the field corn crop feeds the cattle, pigs, and chickens that provide Americans with their bountiful supply of meat, milk, and eggs. Another large percentage is exported: the U.S. produces over 40% of the world's corn and provides over 80% of the world trade in corn. About 2% of the national corn production is processed by the dry milling industry into cornmeal, corn flour, and grits. These are further processed into breakfast cereals, snacks, baked goods, and a number of industrial products. Most of the remainder, approximately 15% of the total corn crop last year, is used by the corn-refining industry to produce a rapidly widening array of products with economic, environmental, and nutritional benefits.

  Each kernel of corn is made up of a seed coat (endosperm) and embryo (germ). The seed coat is the source of bran. The endosperm is composed of 90% starch and 7% gluten or protein.

  The germ contains 40 to 50% oil. In corn refining plants, corn is separated into these components and processed further. Corn-refining technology unlocks the treasure within each kernel.

Starch

Starch, one of nature's major renewable resources, is at the foundation of our food and industrial economy. Starches are used as surface finishes for textiles and papers, and as adhesives. Thousands of ready-to-eat foods depend on starch to give them the desired texture. An exciting new role for cornstarches is in the production of industrial chemicals and plastics which at present come mostly from petroleum. This role will undoubtedly increase in importance as our non-renewable supplies of petroleum are depleted or become less reliable.

  Much of the starch produced is converted to sugars. Think of a starch molecule as a chain of beads. Each bead is a sugar molecule. Enzymes and/or acids are used to break the starch chain apart into various sugars. The result is corn syrups.

Corn Syrups and Ethanol

Corn syrups have a myriad of uses. They are not just sweeteners; they also prevent crystals from forming in our ice cream and keep the ingredients in our hot dogs evenly suspended. Corn syrups can be further processed into dextrose. Dextrose has many uses in the pharmaceutical, baking, and brewing industries. It is also the starting material in the production of ethanol.

  Ethanol is used in many ways, but the primary demand for it comes from gasoline companies. Fuel ethanol use began as "gasohol," a gasoline extender. Its value has increased as it replaced lead as an octane enhancer. Furthermore, a 10% blend of ethanol in gasoline decreases carbon monoxide production by 25-30%. Ethanol provides us with a renewable, domestic source of fuel that is good for the environment.

  So, you can see, corn is a very versatile crop! It touches our lives in more ways that we can imagine. And, with biologists, chemists, and engineers continually working together to find new ways to use corn, it will undoubtedly play an even bigger role in the future.

ACTIVITIES

Main Concept: Corn is more than a food. Corn-refining technology yields specific products from each part of the kernel. These products are further refined and used in the production of hundreds of things we use every day.

Vocabulary
Answers: 1. margarine, 2. tortilla chips, 3. pudding, 4. soft drink

  Tell students that ingredients are listed in order of their amount in the product from greatest to least.

Weekly Lab
Cornstarch forms many different products, depending on

how much water is added. Students need cornstarch, a container of water, a bowl or flat surface covered with plastic wrap, and a spoon. Have them mix the cornstarch with water. Start with 2 teaspoons of cornstarch. Drops of water can be added using a medicine dropper, straw, or a spoon. They can vary the amount of water to see how that affects the product. Two parts cornstarch to one part water gives a modeling dough consistency. Equal amounts of cornstarch and water gives the consistency of liquid glue. This is a very tactile experience, and mixing with fingers is encouraged. Have students describe how the cornstarch feels with no water, a little water, equal amounts of water, and finally with lots of water. Record the descriptive words (dry, wet, sticky, soft, hard). Let them make shapes with their new products and take them home.

The number of drops of water needed will vary according to humidity, size of drops, and size of spoon. From a 1.2 inch diameter straw, you need approximately 24 drops for the first product, and 6 more for the second product (using one teaspoon of cornstarch).

Have the team make the products sequentially. At first, they can guess the number of drops. Then, based on experience, they can predict. Extend by having them make a third product that looks like liquid glue. Test this "glue's" sticking power. It sticks when wet, but separates when dry. This ability makes it useful in finishing paper and in starching and sizing textiles. Students can also try to dissolve cornstarch in water. Like other starches (e.g., flour) it will not dissolve in water. It forms a suspension.

Weekly Problem
Answers: 1. sweeteners; 2. alcohol; 3. 0.4; 4. 17%

Writing for Science
ECO-FOAM™ is made of 95% starch. The starch has been modified so that it is biodegradable. The starch is non-toxic and safe to be used with food. It can replace petroleum-based packing. Have students think of different uses for ECO-FOAM™ and write ads for them. Let them share their ads with the class. If you have some ECO-FOAM™, let the students experiment with it to get ideas.

ECO-FOAM™ is a cornstarch-based packing material. It is water soluble, and therefore good for the environment. Have the class experiment with ECO-FOAM™ and compare these packing peanuts with the indestructible plastic kind. Order ECO-FOAM™ from American Excelsior Company, P.O. Box 5067, Arlington, TX 76011, Attn: ECO-FOAM™. Enclose a check for $2.50 for postage and handling. You will receive 1 cubic foot of ECO-FOAM™ plus literature about the product.

Challenge
Discuss the concept of supply and demand. Among the factors that can influence supply are weather conditions, acreage planted, and imports. Demand can be affected by discovery of new uses for corn like ethanol, biodegradable plastics, packing foam, and corn substitutes for fat in foods. The commodity market speculates on what will happen in the future.

Puzzle
Answers: Batteries, Chalk, Fireworks, Frosting, Glue, Gum, Jam, Meat, Medicine, Ring, Soap, Straws, Tires

The Potato Conquers Europe

BACKGROUND

Potatoes are not native to North America or Europe. They were first grown in the Andes mountains of South America. Their rise to become one of the world's four main food crops took centuries.

In the early 1500s, Spanish explorers visiting the Andes mountains of modern-day Peru found the advanced civilization of the Incas. The Incas were knowledgeable in agriculture and were growing many crops that had not yet been seen in Europe. Because the ships' stores had run out, the Spaniards were forced to eat these native foods, including the potato. These potatoes were not like the ones we eat today. They were about the size of peanuts and tasted rather bitter. The natives freeze-dried some of the potatoes in the form of *chuno*. This food could keep for years and provided a steady source of food.

As the Spaniards provisioned their ships for the return voyage, the potato found its way into the holds. It became part of the sailors' diets. Any potatoes left over by the time they got back to Europe were planted as a food crop.

The potato was not particularly well received at first in Spain, or later in France after it had been brought across the Pyreness Mountains. Because the potato grew in the ground, it was thought fit for animal consumption only. In a surprisingly short amount of time, some of Europe's livestock were eating potatoes on a regular basis. However, humans would eat it only when they had nothing else.

Frequent wars in Europe changed that forever. Pillaging armies would devour all the food in sight and loot what they couldn't eat. However, the edible portion of the potato was hidden in the ground and was safe from the ravaging armies. After the armies departed, there was always one source of food unharmed: the potato. The people were forced to eat them and they soon became an important staple in the human diet. Their popularity spread rapidly throughout the rest of Europe and also to the British Isles.

By the early 1700s, potatoes were sent from England to Bermuda as a gift. Visiting colonists from Jamestown requested some potatoes to take with them as a staple for their own colony. At that point, the potato had completed its journey half way around the world and back.

By the mid 1800s, the potato had become an extremely important staple in Europe and Britain. Given the soil

TEACHING NOTES

and climate of Northern Europe, no other crop produces as many calories per acre. In Ireland, the potato was virtually the only food consumed. This almost total dependence on one food crop was an invitation to disaster. Since potatoes don't last as long in storage as grains, a population depending wholly on the potato risks disaster in the event of crop failure. That is what happened in Ireland. In the mid 1840s, a blight developed in the potato crop and within a few years spread to all of Europe and the British Isles. The damage was so severe in Ireland that a million people died and another million fled the country, mostly to the New England region of North America.

The Irish took their beloved potato with them and rebuilt the potato crop from a few resistant strains.

From this sad episode, two good things resulted. One is that people learned never to depend on one crop. The second is that the potato became a major food staple in North America thanks to the Irish.

The potato helped many nations industrialize. The potato produced much more nutrition per acre and fewer farms could feed more people. This helped Germany and Russia become industrial nations and world powers. Acceptance of the potato helped change the world forever.

ACTIVITIES

Main Concept: Spanish explorers found the potato in South America. They brought it to Europe where it was slowly accepted as a staple crop. Settlers then brought it to North America.

Vocabulary
Have the children use a dictionary to check their answers. See if they can make plurals of other words ending in "o."

Weekly Lab
Students will observe that cutting a potato into many pieces and planting each separately will generate many more pounds of potatoes than just planting a whole potato in one location. If you wish to continue this project, flower pots will not be large enough for each plant to develop a complete crop of potatoes. You will need about a bushel of dirt for each plant.

Weekly Problem
Answer: The distance from Peru to Spain. 10,620.

Challenge
Answer: opinion, fact, opinion, opinion, fact

What kept Europeans from eating the potato at first, fact or opinion? Are there other examples of when people confuse fact with opinion?

Puzzle

2	8	8	6
10	2	5	7
4	6	9	5
8	8	2	6

Potatoes Today

BACKGROUND

This section on the potato looks at the nutritious content of what has been called the world's most perfect food. The potato is a nutrient-dense food, meaning it gives the consumer a lot of nutrition for a small number of calories. It is also very economical, costing only pennies per serving. After slow acceptance in Europe, the potato has become one of the world's favorite and most important foods. Today its uses vary from country to country. In the United States, potatoes are primarily used as food for people. This country produces over 15 million tons of potatoes each year, mostly in Idaho and Washington. Americans eat more potatoes that any other food. They are second only to milk in consumption. In other countries, potatoes are fed to livestock. Like corn, the potato also has a number of uses in manufacturing.

The potato's rich carbohydrates make it a valuable food. Carbohydrates make up 15% (by net weight) of the potato and provide long term fuel for the body. The potato's complex carbohydrates can slowly release energy that lasts many hours. In contrast, simple carbohydrates like sugars give a brief burst of energy and then leave the eater feeling listless.

The potato is a good source of vitamin C—second only to the orange. One serving can provide one-half of a person's daily requirement. The potato is also loaded with trace minerals and nutrients. Potatoes contain riboflavin, thiamin, and niacin.

Vitamins are found throughout the potato. However, in preparing potatoes, it is important to remember that most of those vitamins and minerals are just below the skin level so peeling the potato reduces its food value.

Since vitamin C is water soluble, the baked potato, eaten skin and all, is probably the most nutritious method of preparation. Boiling with the skin on is second best. French-fried potatoes and potato chips are lower in vitamins and minerals but still provide complex carbohydrates.

It is also important to store potatoes properly. They should be removed from any packaging right away. Potatoes are living organisms and need air. Store them in a cool, dry place, preferably where they will not rest against one another. They should not be refrigerated. Storing them below 40 degrees Fahrenheit will make the carbohydrates turn into sugar. Storing them in very warm temperatures can encourage sprouting and shriveling (between 45 and 50 degrees is ideal). Too much light can cause potatoes to turn green and taste bitter.

The potato offers a lot for the future, too. Scientists are working to develop a potato seed that will be as reliable as potato eyes for growing uniform potatoes. Currently, it takes almost 2,000 kilograms of tuber eyes to plant about 2.5 acres. Recent tests in Peru showed that 120 grams of seeds will plant the same area. Seeds are cheaper and easier to manage than the tubers.

Scientists are also working to develop a more disease-resistant variety of potatoes that will grow well in dry, tropical countries where many people have inadequate diets. Wherever the potato has gone, it has increased the health and energy of the people who adopted it as part of their diet. Because the potato is an adequate and reliable food source, it has also lead to an increase in population.

Potatoes have many non-food uses. They are used in producing gasohol, a fuel alternative, and potato starch is widely used in industry. There is potato ice cream and a potato handcream. Leftover peelings from processed potatoes make biodegradable plastic bags. Together with corn, the potato can be thought of as the true gold shared with Europe and the rest of the world by Columbus and other explorers.

ACTIVITIES

Main Concept: Potatoes are an almost perfect food and one of the most important foods in the world. Scientists are working to find new ways to grow and use the potato.

Vocabulary
Answers: 1. carbohydrates, 2. proteins, 3. potassium, 4. calcium, 5. minerals, 6. vitamins

Weekly Lab
Make sure the ends of the wire are scraped. You can scrape them with a clean penny. The juice in the potato acts as an electrolyte. It carries electricity in the potato, but reacts at different rates with the iron nail and the copper wire. This causes a difference in voltage. You can hear this potential difference as static with the earphones. Try sliding the earphone wires along the wire and nail.

The electrolytic solution in the potato has charged ions. These ions attack the copper wire and the result is more ions. These ions then come together and make a salt. Salts are formed from charged ions. (For example, table salt is sodium chloride—positive sodium ions and negative chlorine ions held together.) The green color you see near the copper wire is evidence of the formation of a copper salt. (Copper salts are usually green or blue.) The gas bubbles are hydrogen gas, another product of this reaction. You can try inert (unreactive) wires (such as platinum) and still get a color (pale pink). This is caused by the action of oxygen (in the air) on the potato. This is the same reaction that causes the potato to brown. It can be slowed by coating the potato with something that will react with the oxygen more easily than the potato (like vitamin C). Lemon juice, which contains vitamin C, will do this. This is why people sprinkle vitamin C, or ascorbic acid, on potatoes before canning them.

Weekly Problem
The average American eats about 60 kilograms of pota-toes in one year. The students could convert this number to pounds.

Challenge
You can buy a "potato clock" through science supply houses or in some toy stores. The clock runs off two pota-toes or other foods (such as lemons).

Puzzle
Answers: Across: 1. peanut, 2. avocado, 3. sugar, 4. tomato; Down: 5. chuno, 6. cacao, 7. corn. 8. potato

The peanut, avocado, tomato, cacao bean, corn, pota-to, and sugar are all native to the Americas. They were exchanged between the hemispheres as a result of Columbus's voyage.

Microconquistadors

BACKGROUND

In the 400 years after Columbus's voyage, native popula-tions in the Americas declined by as much as 90%. During the same period, the population in Africa, Europe, and Asia increased dramatically. An explanation for this can be found in the seeds of change. Columbus and those who followed him unintentionally brought many diseases that Native Americans had never seen before. In return, they took back to Europe corn and the potato, two foods that helped people and countries grow strong.

Although there were many contributing factors to the decline in the Native American population after 1492, the single most important factor was infectious disease. The Americas were not free of disease in the time before Columbus. There is much evidence of a variety of dis-eases. However, because of the isolation of the two hemi-spheres, few diseases were common to both sides of the globe. This meant that the Native Americans had not built up any immunity to the European and African diseases which crossed the Atlantic. Smallpox, measles, and typhus came from Europe; malaria and yellow fever came from Africa. When Native Americans were exposed to these new diseases, nearly everyone was infected at the same time. The diseases spread rapidly and many natives died.

Disease may have traveled in the other directions as well. Columbus may have taken syphilis back with him to Europe. This issue has been debated for centuries. Some say there is no evidence of syphilis in Europe before 1492. There does seem to have been an epidemic of syphilis shortly after Columbus and his men returned. New laboratory techniques may be able to resolve this question.

An early example of the exchange of disease happened in 1493. Within days of Columbus's arrival in Hispaniola (present day Haiti and the Dominican Republic), many natives contracted a respiratory disease and died.

Columbus established his first permanent colony there at Santo Domingo. He brought many things to the island, including grape vines for wine-making. But he also probably brought the smallpox germ. By 1600, there was not one native left on the island.

We don't know how many natives died in all, but estimates range from 60,000 to 8 million. One eyewitness, Bartolome de las Casas, a Dominican friar, later wrote that 3 million natives died within about 10 years of Columbus's arrival. "Who of those in future centuries will believe this? I myself who am writing this and saw it and know the most about it can hardly believe that such was possible."

Disease quickly spread from the islands to the mainland. One soldier may have been responsible for bringing smallpox to the Aztecs. He reportedly stayed with an Aztec family and may have given them the germ. The disease spread rapidly weakening the people. Meanwhile, Hernan Cortes dreamed of conquering the Aztec empire and claiming all the gold and glory it had to offer. When the battle for the Aztec empire began, Cortes faced more than a million Aztecs with only 750 men. He had guns and horses they didn't have, but it was disease that allowed him to conquer easily. The most powerful people in Mesoamerica had been brought down.

There were other conquests. When Francisco Pizarro came to South America to conquer the Incas, he found a land in turmoil. A civil war had occurred six years earlier. Scientists think that a smallpox epidemic may have been one of the causes. The weakened condition of the natives and their leaders made it much easier for Pizarro to conquer the great Incan empire.

There were many epidemics that swept the Americas after Columbus. Sometimes the disease got there before the explorers. Many Native Americans died without ever seeing a European. There are stories of explorers coming into Native American villages and finding everyone dead. Sometimes Native Americans unintentionally spread diseases from one tribe to the next. The effects of the devastation caused by these diseases went on for centuries. Some tribes saw their population continue to decline into the twentieth century. Some tribes never recovered.

Today, we have vaccinations to protect us from specific diseases. Vaccines are made from the dead form, or a live but harmless form, of a specific microbe. Once the vaccine is made, it is given to a patient in the form of an injection or a drink. The vaccine causes the person's body to make memory cells for that particular microbe. If the real microbe ever invades that person's body, it is destroyed. The ability to fight these microbes is known as immunity. A person who has been given a vaccine has active immunity to that particular disease.

Immunization programs today cover many of the dangerous infectious diseases. These programs are only effective if the whole population gets them. There are areas in the United States in which the immunization of young children is low. Consequently, there have been outbreaks of measles, mumps, and whooping cough in the past years. There are some diseases for which we do not yet have a vaccine. AIDS is an example of a disease that started in one part of the world and then spread rapidly because of the lack of a vaccine. Microconquistadors are not a thing of the past.

ACTIVITIES

Main Concept: Diseases brought to America by European explorers had a devastating effect on the natives. Today we have vaccines to give us immunity to specific diseases. Vaccines do this by stimulating the body to produce memory cells. Memory cells help destroy disease-causing microbes.

Vocabulary
Answers: 1. vaccine, 2. immunization, 3. germs, 4. immunity, 5. microbes. Secret word: virus

Weekly Lab
Infections may spread rapidly because one person with the infection may pass the infection on to many other people. One method of stopping infection is vaccination. Antibiotics, which will be discussed in the next issue, are chemicals given to stop the growth of microbes.

Weekly Problem
Four germs will exist after one hour. Sixteen germs will exist after two hours.

Writing for Science
You might ask the students some leading questions. Would settlers have been able to take Native American land? Would there be large numbers of Native Americans in the United States? Would we have treated the environment differently? Would there be powerful tribal nations in America?

Challenge
Students can make educated guesses. Have them try a sixth drop to see how close their guess came. If several students do this, they will probably see that they all come up with different results.

Puzzle
Answers: measles, mumps, tetanus

Cures and Carriers

BACKGROUND

"I believe the islands contain many herbs and many trees which will be worth a great amount in Spain for dyes and as medicinal spices, but I do not recognize them and I much regret that."

As the ships of the early explorers left port for the Americas, they carried a carefully chosen selection of goods, livestock, and crewmen. But they also carried many uninvited and sometimes unseen passengers: disease organisms and their carriers.

The Carriers

The primary disease vectors aboard the European ships were the ship's crew. Smallpox was the first epidemic to ravage the American natives. It is estimated that up to 90% of the people in some locations were killed. It is unlikely that a crewman arrived with an active infection, but scabs in unwashed clothing or bandages probably infected the people on shore.

Cholera, typhus, and diphtheria also took their toll within the first three decades after contact. Although the initial infections were probably caused by infected crew members, these microbes spread quickly through the water supply. Malaria microbes probably arrived in the bloodstream of people from Europe or Africa. Malaria is spread from person to person only by the bite of the Anopheles mosquito. Unfortunately, a species of Anopheles mosquito lived in the American tropics. Once exposed to malaria microbes, this mosquito began to spread malaria to both Native Americans and explorers.

Another vector aboard the ships was the European black rat. European cities of the fifteenth century abounded with rats. Ships leaving port always carried a few stowaways. It was not the rats themselves that transmitted plague, but the fleas that lived on them. Like malaria, plague is transmitted by an insect bite. When the rats died, the fleas moved to humans and infected them with plague.

Livestock animals, such as cattle, swine, and horses, also brought disease. Once these animals became part of the local agricultural practice, tuberculosis, influenza, and other illnesses were incubated in the animals and passed to humans through meat, dairy products, and animal wastes in water supplies.

The Cures

The medical expertise of the Europeans and Native Americans was limited by their lack of understanding about the origins of disease. The lack of antiseptic conditions during treatments like bloodletting or amputations meant that most patients died of post-operative infection. However, greater numbers of Native American patients survived than European ones. Native American healers had discovered several effective drug treatments which they made from local plants. Journals suggest that many sailors preferred to be treated by native healers than by the barber-physicians that usually came on the ships.

The most important herbal cure developed by the natives was quinine for malaria. The native healers showed the Europeans how to boil the bark of the *cinchona* (sin-KO-na) tree to extract the quinine. Quinine can now be made synthetically, but some strains of malaria respond only to the herbal extract.

Another herbal cure commonly in use during that time was cocaine. It was an effective anesthetic when extracted from the leaves. The natives also chewed it for energy. Although cocaine is an illegal drug, doctors today can use it for eye surgery. Its cousin, novocaine, is used in dentistry.

There are many other important and powerful drugs from the American forests: cascara sagrada is a laxative made from the bark of a tree which grows on the western coast of North America; ipecac, made from the roots of a jungle tree in South America, is used for amoebic dysentery as well as for accidental poisonings; curare, used for tipping poisoned arrows, is a powerful muscle relaxant when used in small quantities.

Recently, the bark of the yew tree, long considered a trash tree by loggers and foresters, has been found to contain an important anti-cancer drug. Forestry people are now concerned that the yew will be wiped out to make pharmaceutical drugs and are taking steps to protect it from extinction.

Fortunately, most herbal remedies can be made in the lab now, saving many rare plants from extinction. But scientists are worried that with the decline of the world's tropical rain forests we are losing many potential sources of cures for the illnesses that trouble us today.

ACTIVITIES

Main Concept: Germs are spread in many ways. Native Americans knew about some natural cures. Today, medicines and good health practices can stop the spread of disease. However, there are no cures for some diseases.

Vocabulary
Answers: a. fever, b. vector, c. quinine, d. microbe, e. antibiotic, f. cure

Weekly Lab
Make sure students wait overnight before doing step 3. Most microbes will grow in areas that are handled a great deal—bathrooms, water fountains, pens, etc. The least growth will occur in a place which is kept clean and is not frequently handled.

Weekly Problem
Answers: 9 seconds, 36 seconds
Ask the students what information in the problem is not needed. (The fact that a sneeze can carry as many as 100,000 microbes.) You may want them to create a problem using this information.

Writing for Science
If the children are having difficulty, some methods of stopping the spread of disease could be listed on the board. The students would then be responsible for using this information to write the notices.

Students can plan special events for the town meeting—a demonstration on purifying water, a talk from the newly elected sanitation chief, a model of a cean house, etc.

Challenge
Let students talk out how they solved the problem.

Puzzle
Answers: e, 2,832; i, 2,610; p, 2,484; l, 2,790; n, 2,664; g, 2,703

"Fizgig" was the word people used to describe a dizzy person. "Pingle" meant to eat without much appetite. "Sloomy" meant sleepy. "Turngiddy" was a word for dizzy. These and other popular words from times past can be found in *Murfles and Wink-a-Peeps: Funny Old Words for Kids* by Susan Kelz Sperling, Clarkson N. Potter, Inc. Publishers, NY, 1985.

The Horse Returns to America

BACKGROUND

The horse was a gift from Europe brought back to the Americas by Columbus on his second voyage. At first, the horse was instrumental in enabling the Spanish to conquer the natives. But, later, when the natives got their own horses, their lifestyles changed to take advantage of the opportunities presented by the horse. The horse was perhaps the greatest benefit the Native Americans received from the exchange.

The Early Horse
Scientists believe that the family of horses originated in North America about 55 million years ago. It migrated over the land bridges and spread throughout Europe and Asia. The earliest horse, called *Eohippus*, or "drawn horse," was a creature about the size of a small dog. It had toes on each foot instead of the hoof we know today. The early horse spread these toes out to keep from sinking into the boggy earth. Its habitat was the jungle-like forest where it hid from its enemies. It munched on the lush leaves, fern fronds, small fruits, and twigs found in this environment.

In time, the inland seas and swamps dried up. Palms were replaced by trees and moss yielded to grass. As the forest gradually gave way to the more open grassland, the horse had to evolve into a grass-grazing animal. Its teeth changed to adapt to the coarser grasses. It also had to gallop over the harder ground of the grasslands. The side toes on its foot gradually disappeared, until the remaining middle toe became one horny hoof. Along with these changes, horses also increased in size. About ten thousand years before the arrival of Columbus, the horse mysteriously disappeared from the Americas. It was not until

Columbus's second voyage in 1493 that the horse would return to its home. Unknowingly, Columbus brought back to America one of the most important seeds of change to affect humankind.

The Horse in the Americas
In 1519, Herman Cortes brought the first horses to the North American mainland when he landed in Mexico. They were instrumental in his victory over the Aztec empire. Next to disease, the horse was the greatest enemy of the Aztecs. Cortes once said he valued one horse to 20 men. Mexico became a breeding ground for horses in North America. The horses bred prolifically here and spread from Mexico northward into what is now the southwestern United States and Great Plains area. The grass remembered this native animal and the horse thrived on the grasslands. In South America, Peru was the breeding ground. Horses spread from here to Bolivia, Chile, Paraguay, Uruguay, and Argentina.

Although the natives were terrified of what this giant animal could do in war, they soon learned to appreciate the power and the beauty of this wondrous animal as much as the Spanish did. As the Native Americans got their own horses, their way of life changed. Before the horse, they had to hunt on foot or drive large animals off cliffs to kill them. The nomadic tribes walked and used dogs to pull their possessions. The wheel was unknown. Some scientists speculate this was because the Native North Americans had no domesticated animal large enough to pull a wheeled vehicle, making a wheel unnecessary.

A Changing Lifestyle
The horse allowed the native to hunt larger and faster game. The people became better fed and stronger. The horse could carry a larger load allowing people to acquire more possessions and travel greater distances. Elderly and weak people no longer had to fear being left behind when the tribe moved on.

The Plains tribes of America were particularly affected. Now they could travel with the great buffalo herds, migrating with their food supply and the change of seasons. The hunting was so good that some tribes who had planted crops became nomadic. Although the importance of the horse as a work animal and beast of burden has diminished, it is still easy to see the importance the horse plays in the lives of many people. The people of the Americas have once again claimed the horse as their own.

ACTIVITIES

Main Concept: The horse originated in North America, mysteriously disappearing 10,000 years ago. It evolved over the course of millions of years to what it is today. Columbus brought the horse back to America on his second voyage.

Vocabulary

Students may be able to point out other parts of the horse (e.g., hoof, chest, hip, and thigh). Get a picture that shows the parts of the horse and compare.

Weekly Lab

Fossils may be remains of animals or impressions in clay which have turned to stone. The fossils of the earliest horse would be found in the lowest or deepest deposits. The different colors of clay represent the different types of soil deposits. Students may not know what fossils are.

By noting and comparing these types of soil, archaeologists can make a match with known deposits and known time periods. This would help alleviate the problems caused by geological upheaval (earthquakes and erosion).

Weekly Problem

The earliest horse measured about 30 cm, 300 mm, .3 m. The modern horse measures about 150 cm, 1500 mm, 1.5 m.

Writing for Science

Students could pick a specific tribe and do research on how the horse changed their lives. See the background notes for more information.

Challenge

The original horse comes first, then the horse spreading across the land bridge, then the tame horse and, last, the present-day horse. Students may add when the horse disappeared and when Columbus brought the horse back to America on their timelines.

Puzzle

The footprints with the shorter stride and the full foot down shows an animal walking. The footprints with the longer stride and just part of the foot down shows an animal running. Compare with what children see in real life. The running animal caught up with the walking one and may have eaten it. This shows how important the ability to gallop was to the survival of the horse. Students may be able to see why the foot had to change so the horse could run fast.

The Horse in America

BACKGROUND

The horse has always played an important role in the conquest and settlement of people and land, but probably never as much as it did in America.

The Spanish Bring Ranching to America

The cowboy's life that we associate with the Old American West (round-ups, branding, cattle drives, and hours in the saddle) was actually developed in Spain during medieval times. The Spanish brought this lifestyle with them to America. The vast grasslands of North and South America were ideal for cattle and horses.

Mexico proved to be an excellent country for grazing stock. The Spanish imported a sturdy range cow which eventually became the backbone of the American ranching industry. They also bred horses in Mexico and sent them north to the American Southwest and Great Plains. Along with the horse, the Spanish idea of ranching spread to the Southwest.

Horses and Native Americans

At first, the Spanish did not want Native Americans to have horses. They wanted to keep the extra power that the horse gave them to themselves. But, eventually, the herds of cattle got so big that the Spanish had to train Native Americans to use horses so they could help the Spanish work the herds. Native Americans, realizing they had to get their own horses, caught or stole them. In 1680, the Pueblo Revolt near Santa Fe, New Mexico, enabled Native Americans to capture or set free thousands of Spanish horses. Within 100 years, all the Native American groups west of the Mississippi had horses.

The horse brought many changes to the lifestyles of the Native Americans. They no longer had to carry heavy burdens. They could hunt buffalo on horseback, instead of chasing them over cliffs.

Now they could kill only what they needed. Some tribes abandoned farming for hunting and following the herd. The horse took on a central importance and even religious significance in many tribes.

Farming and Industry in the East

People who came to settle the American East brought the European concept of farming with them. They set up small farms with fields of crops and a few farm animals such as cows, chickens, and pigs. The horse helped them plow the land, ship their goods, and take them from farm to farm and into town.

Horses also helped power the businesses and industries in the East. The first crude motors were often driven by men, oxen, or horses turning a wheel. Some scientists believe that the wheel was not known in the pre-Columbian Americas because the people did not have a domesticated animal large enough to pull a wheeled vehicle.

The horse also provided the primary means of early transportation for raw materials, products, and people. The horse-drawn streetcar was one of the first means of public transportation. When the automobile, or horseless carriage, was invented, its power was measured in horsepower, a term we still use.

Westward Expansion

The East became too crowded for some people and they decided to pack their belongings and head out to the seemingly limitless lands in the West. At first, wagons were hitched to oxen. But the oxen were slow compared to the horse. The horse was also more versatile once the settlers got to their land. Soon, horses replaced the oxen in wagon trains.

Easterners set up farms once they got to the West. They built fences around their land as they had done in the east. However, cattle ranchers were used to letting their herds roam the grasslands to graze. Ranching and farming seemed incompatible and bitter fights broke out. Eventually, ranchers realized that fences could keep their herds in smaller areas and round-ups were no longer needed. The invention of the plow and the water pump helped ranchers grow more corn to use for cattle feed. Cattle did not have to graze anymore. The railroad, or "Iron Horse," that had brought many settlers to the West, could also be used to transport cattle and beef. Technology brought an end to the age of the cowboy.

ACTIVITIES

Main Concept: The Spanish set up large ranches after they conquered the native people in Central and South America. From here, the horse spread to North America. Horses helped bring about many changes in farming, ranching, industry, and transportation.

Vocabulary
Other horse expressions are: in the saddle again, backing the wrong horse, horsing around, be on one's high horse, hold one's horses, and a horse of another color. Point out to students that the horse has been so important in our history that we have made it part of our language.

Weekly Lab
Have students experiment with levers and other simple machines. Ask them what other forms of energy were used to power mill and other businesses. Possible answers are water and wind.

Weekly Problem
Answer: 6 horses, 15 horses, 10.5 horses, 45 horses

The definition of 1 horsepower has changed from time to time. This figure is one value.

Writing for Science
Some arguments for fences: fences protect farm crops, they mark land boundaries, and they keep cattle from trampling the farm land. Some arguments against fences: fences prevent cattle from getting all the food they need, they hurt cattle who brush against the barbed wire, they prevent cattle from getting to watering holes.

Challenge
There is more than one correct answer for the first part:
4 carriage horses
1 cow pony + 2 carriage horses
1 cow pony + 1 carriage horse + 2 plow horses
2 carriage horses + 4 plow horses
1 carriage horse + 6 plow horses

Challenge students to come up with as many different combinations as possible. The greatest number of horses you can get if you have to buy at least one cow pony is five: 1 cow pony and 4 plow horses.

Puzzle
The Chisholm Trail has 8 letters. The Pony Express operated for 18 months (April 30, 1960 – October 24, 1861). Barbed wire was patented in 1873. The Golden Spike was driven in on May 10, 1869. The total of the 3 smallest numbers (8, 18, and 10) is 36. 36 divided by 3 is 12. 12 – 1 = 11. Add 11 to 1873, you get 1884, the year the first organized rodeo opened in Pecos, Texas.

Down on the Farm

BACKGROUND

Newcomers in America
Before the arrival of Columbus, Native Americans did not have the types of domesticated livestock that we commonly think of as farm and ranch animals. They farmed on small plots of land and were careful to stay in harmony with the environment. The arrival of the Europeans and their animals drastically changed American agricultural practices.

When the Spanish arrived in America, they found that they did not like the local food and they became homesick for the tastes and types of food from their homeland. On his second voyage in 1493, Columbus brought not only the horse and cow, but also seeds and cuttings of many plants as well as a variety of animals, including dogs, pigs, chickens, sheep, and goats. These animals changed the way America was farmed.

The animals landed in the Antilles and formed the basis for the stock that would later be taken to the mainland. The livestock did well in the Antilles where there were few large predators, no local deadly diseases, and plenty of food. The back country soon swarmed with wild animals that had escaped, providing later Spanish armies with plenty of livestock for their soldiers to eat. When Hernando de Soto took hundreds of pigs on his journeys, it is likely that they were descendants from the original eight that Columbus imported.

These new animals soon made their mark on the land. By the seventeenth century, there were reports that cattle and horses were so numerous in parts of South America that they were destroying the ground cover. Similar problems were encountered with the goats and sheep. The pigs represented a slightly different problem since they not only rooted up local food crops but even ate some of the local wildlife.

Conflicts Between Ranching and Farming
The European settlers plowed and planted large tracts of land. Often, they had a single crop which exposed the soil

to erosion. Their way of farming was completely opposite to the way Native Americans farmed. The land began to change because of what people were doing.

As ranching and farming spread, there were other problems. In the East, where there was a tradition of crop farming with a limited amount of livestock, people were used to fencing land to control the animals. In the grasslands of the West and pampas of South America, there was a tradition of open land where cattle and horses roamed freely. Fierce fighting broke out when the farmers began to move westward. Naturally, they needed to fence their land to keep the wandering cattle from destroying their crops. Cattle, on the other hand, required increasingly large amounts of grass and needed free access to the range. They undoubtedly looked upon the crops as a free and convenient meal. Part of our Western tradition is the story of the great range wars that resulted from this conflict of interests. Folk legends such as Billy the Kid and Sheriff Pat Garrett have their roots in the Lincoln County range wars.

Eventually people began to realize that corn-fed cattle grew much larger and tastier than grazing cattle. In addition, the ranges were becoming so overgrazed that it took hundreds of acres just to feed a few cattle on grass. Ranchers began letting the cattle graze on grass for a while, then brought them into a small area to feed them hay and grain to fatten them for market. The ranchers started to build their own fences to keep their cattle near the food source.

The Need for Land Management
We are only beginning to understand the consequences that the introduction of the large farm animals had on the American ecosystem. The lesson that the ranchers learned is that we must manage our resources if we want them to last. Farmers practice land management when they rotate their crops and fertilize their fields. Bad land management through overplanting and poor plowing methods exhausted the land in Oklahoma in the 1930s.

When there was a drought we were left with the Great Oklahoma Dust Bowl. Farmers lost their land and people starved. Today, ranching in Central and South America is the major cause of the destruction of tropical rain forests. However, renewed awareness of the fragility of our resources has made many of us more careful with how we use them. Being careless with our natural resources can result in disaster.

ACTIVITIES

Main Concept: The animals Columbus brought with him changed the land. People let the animals run free over the grasslands until the land was damaged. Now, farmers practice land management to conserve our resources.

Vocabulary
Answers: domesticated, tamed; thrived; flourish or increase; conquered, overthrow; cultivate, to plow or fertilize; inexhaustible, incapable of being used up; colonized, to migrate to and settle in

Weekly Lab
Repeat the experiment and vary the number of horses, cattle, and danger squares. Have the students keep track of the differences they notice. Ask them how they can make the resources last longer.

Weekly Problem
Lisa will need 362 yards of fencing. Use the word "perimeter" with the students when discussing the amount of fencing needed. The land is 7,260 square meters, or 1.6 acres. 1 acre = 4404.4 square meters. (Note that the measure is acre and not square acre, since the definition of acre is a square measure.)

Writing for Science
Students may need to do some research to find out what is going on in farming today. Have them start with the newspaper.

Challenge
Answers: 1. having the teacher reject their papers, 2. trying out for the farmer's newsletter, 3. oversleeping and forgetting to do assignments, 4. 1/3 + 1/6 or 1/6 + 1/4 + 1/12

Puzzle
It takes one hen 3 days to lay one egg. One hen in 300 days can lay 100 eggs. Three hundred hens in 300 days can lay 300 x 100 eggs, or 30,000 eggs.

Archaeology

BACKGROUND

"Galways—for 250 years—operated as a settlement, an economic unit, an industrial enterprise, a resource management system, a part of a world-wide system of colonial trade, a stratified social community, and a transmitter of culture."

Within 50 years of Columbus's second voyage, the European demand for sugar cane led to a sugar plantation-based economy in the Caribbean. Slavery and the destruction of the tropical rainforest in the Western Hemisphere were two tragic results. The plantation became part of a transatlantic economic system involving sugar, money, and slaves. The sugar cane plantation was both agricultural and industrial in nature since it processed sugar as well as grew sugar cane. The philosophy of the times was to subdue nature, and mine the wealth of the "New World" by growing as much sugar cane as possible using enforced labor. Recent archaeological study of Galways Plantation on Montserrat paints a picture of daily life in the 18th century.

History of Montserrat

Montserrat is a volcanic island, only 7 miles long and 5 miles wide at 17 degrees above the equator. On his second voyage in 1493, Columbus named the island without ever landing on it. But it was on this second voyage that he introduced sugar cane to Santo Domingo. Sugar had come to the Caribbean because of the climate, and it thrived in the tropical environment.

By 1632, British and Irish Catholics founded a colony on Montserrat to escape religious and political persecution. Initially, they grew indigo and cotton on small plots. Land previously shared in common by Native Americans was subdivided and registered to individual owners. Larger holdings were consolidated, and tobacco became the cash crop until sugar was introduced to this island in 1650. In less than 50 years, two-thirds of the rain forest was destroyed for fields of sugar cane.

Sugar cane is a labor-intensive crop. After a while there were no longer sufficient indentured Irish servants to provide the necessary labor. Traders brought slaves to the island in exchange for the sugar that they took to Europe. Africans shared many immunities with the Europeans, which enabled them to resist disease better than Native Americans.

The 1678 census reported a few hundred English, several thousand Irish, and 992 Africans. Over time, the social structure changed to an Anglo-Irish planter class with a slave population that grew until blacks outnumbered whites. While planters celebrated St. Patrick's Day in 1768, the slaves rebelled. This slave resistance and rebellion is commemorated on the island today. Slavery was outlawed during the 1800s. After 1809, it was illegal for someone to buy another human being. Today, 90% of the population of Montserrat is black with West African origins, yet many speak with an Irish brogue, have Irish surnames, and live on what is nicknamed the Emerald Isle of the Caribbean. They celebrate St. Patrick's Day with fife, drum, and folk dances.

The larger islands of the Caribbean continued to be major sugar growers in the 20th century. However, Galways was abandoned as a settlement sometime after the 1860s, or about 200 years after it was first settled by the English. By the 1970s, much of Galways had returned to vine-covered jungles.

The Dig at Galways

Archaeologists paint a picture of how people lived long ago. They work together with historians and other scientists to fill in gaps in our knowledge of the past.

The Galways project led by Dr. Lydia M. Pulsipher, a geographer at the University of Tennessee, and Dr. Conrad M. Goodwin, an archaeologist, began in 1979 at the request of the Montserrat National Trust. In 1988, the Smithsonian Institution selected it to be a part of the Seeds of Change exhibit. Galways provides a case study of the effects of introducing sugar to the Americas. Many teachers and students have participated in summer "digs" over the past 10 years.

Land records indicated that Galways Plantation was founded in the 1600s by David Galways. The plantation operated for about 200 years until it fell into ruin. Over the past 10 years, the stone ruins of Galways have been cleared of vegetation, surveyed, and mapped. After searching the site looking for surface findings, archaeologists decided where to dig. They also took aerial photographs.

Before excavating, archaeologists mark the surface with a grid system 5 feet square. They shave each layer of dirt off with a pointed trowel. Each finding is brushed, washed, numbered, and classified according to its type, position, and depth. Dirt is sifted to locate small pieces. Each finding is a piece of a puzzle. Artifacts are those findings made by humans. Archaeologists ask, "Who made this?" and "How did they use it?"

Slave Village

The last three years of digging have focused on excavating the slave village area of Galways. In 1677, 74 slaves lived on the plantation. Since the slave houses were made of wood and palm leaves, they have been destroyed and recycled by nature. But we know what they look like from writings and drawings of the 1800s.

People of the island help the researchers in uncovering their history. Bits of bone, pieces of china, seeds, metal graters, and griddles are a few of the clues of the slaves' daily life. Dishes and tools from China, England, and North America found at the site illustrate how this plantation was tied to the larger world.

The Africans learned from the natives how to farm in the rain forest left at the top of the mountains. In these secret gardens they were able to grow food and enjoy brief moments of independence. Slaves depended on imported food. Slaves grew maize, peanuts, cassava, pineapple, sweet potatoes, peppers, squash, guavas, avocados, beans, and medicinal plants. The number of discovered metal graters and griddles for making flat disks of cassava bread suggest that this was done to produce income for the slaves. Laws established to control slave activities give further evidence of slaves' entrepreneurial skills at the Sunday markets. Through hard work, resistance to slave owners' demands, and at times, open rebellion, the enslaved people demonstrated their resourcefulness despite constant hardship.

ACTIVITIES

Main Concept: Sugar plantations prospered using enslaved labor. The enslaved Africans developed their own community life. Archaeologists help us find out about the past.

Weekly Lab

Prepare dig boxes for each item. Line cardboard boxes with plastic bags and fill halfway with sand or dirt. Mix in an assortment of 'artifacts': old toys, broken pieces of foam plates or cups, broken pencils, coins, etc. You can also include things such as seed pods, nuts, raisins, popcorn seeds, and rocks. Try to avoid sharp objects; however, if you think your students will be careful, broken pottery is very interesting. Caution the students to be careful in their search because they do not know if they will encounter something sharp. Ask students to reassemble broken items. Spoons can be used instead of trowels. Old toothbrushes are fine. Cover work areas with newspaper. Sieves are optional. They are useful for finding small objects.

Label coordinates for each section of the grid as follows: (A,1); (A,2); (B,1); (B,2). A code number might be C1-(A,1)-10 meaning coin number one found in grid space (A,1) at a depth of 10 cm. Have students form teams of diggers, sorters, labelers, and recorders. Older objects are usually found at deeper spots in a real dig. An artifact is something made by humans. Students may have to revise their classification systems because they may not have identified a type of object or may have too broad a category. Alternate sites to explore are the school cafeteria floor after lunch and the classroom floor.

Weekly Problem

Answers: 1678 = 1/4, 1729 = 5/6. Ask students if they notice a change in the proportions of the population. English settlers tended to move on to new fields in Jamaica and other large islands once the soil became depleted. Many Irish servants, once their indenture period was over, left the island. So plantations became more dependent on bringing Africans; it was also more profitable because they were not paid labor.

Writing for Science

Discuss how a piece of historical fiction that the class has read weaves fact and fiction together to make a story. An archaeologist also tries to tell a story. Students might make the statement, "Jennifer loved candy canes," after finding something with the name Jennifer in the bag and also finding part of a candy cane. But can we know that for sure? Maybe it's more accurate to say, "Jennifer had a candy cane, or there were candy canes where Jennifer lived."

Challenge

Answers: (50 meter x 80 meters) – (20 meters x 20 meters) = 360 square meters

Puzzle

Across: 1. load, 3. program, 7. bug, 8. monitor, 9. cursor
Down: 1. loop, 2. computer, 4. run, 5. menu, 6. boot

Sugar

BACKGROUND

There is a huge demand for sugar in the world today. The world produces about 97 million tons of sugar annually. Cuba, Brazil, and India are the leaders in sugar cane production, while the USSR, France, West Germany, and the United States grow the most sugar beets. The sugar industry creates jobs for many people on farms, in sugar factories, and in the transportation of the finished product.

Some of us are even wearing sugar or its by-products. Sugar is sometimes used for treating cloth to make it crease-resistant. It is used in livestock feed, plastics, wallboard, nylon fiber, and many drugs and dyes. There is little waste in sugar production.

We eat all kinds of sugar. Molasses is thick, brown syrup that is left when sugar has crystallized. To make white sugar, molasses is removed from the raw sugar crystals. This process is called refining. Granulated and powered sugar are two types of refined sugar. Brown sugar is made by refining the sugar and then putting back some of the molasses.

Two plants, the sugar cane and sugar beet, supply most of the sugar we consume. Like all plants, they live by absorbing water through their roots, and carbon dioxide and sunlight through their leaves. During this process, known as photosynthesis, these factors combine to form a type of sugar. The sugar supplies plants with their energy.

Many historians feel that the sugar cane was the plant most responsible for the establishment of slavery in the Americas. The demand for labor in the West Indies sugar cane plantations led to the importation of Africans to work in the fields. In time these plantations replaced the tropical rain forests in that area. In earlier years sugar cane production harmed both human beings and the environment.

The United States leads the world in sugar consumption. Health experts have suggested that we cut our sugar intake by as much as 50 percent. One government survey showed that 98 percent of children in the United States have some tooth decay.

There are many ways to reduce the intake of refined sugar. People should eat more starches and natural sugars in the form of more fruits, vegetables, and grain products. We should also consume fewer soft drinks and avoid processed food with high amounts of sugar. Finally, we should read food labels to see if sugar is listed as a primary ingredient.

ACTIVITIES

Main Concept: There is a high consumption of sugar in the United States. Most of the sugar we consume comes from sugar cane and sugar beets. We should monitor the amount of sugar in our diet.

Weekly Lab

An insect's sense of smell and taste may be located in its antenna. Some insects are naturally attracted to water (hydrotropism). Other insects are attracted to or repelled by smell. Try to determine which insects were attracted to each container.

Weekly Problem

Answers: The artificial sweetener is the best buy. You would only need 0.6 kilograms of artificial sweetener. Artificial sweetener would cost $2.60 ($4.33 x 0.6 kilograms). Sugar would cost $7.74 ($2.58 x 3 kilograms).

Writing for Science

Students should use an encyclopedia to research each crop prior to writing. One similarity is that they are both thirsty plants. A sugar beet may take in as much as 15 gallons of water in a growing season.

Challenge

Discuss the difference between temperate climates and tropical climates and how they affect which crop will be grown and where.

Puzzle

The states with warm climates will produce sugar cane. The states with mild climates will produce sugar beets.

Technology

BACKGROUND

In 1492 when Columbus set sail, the words *science* and *technology* were not in his vocabulary, and yet, he made his voyage, in part, because of advances in science and technology. From the first section (Sailing the Ocean Blue) you know that Columbus made use of several sailing instruments, including the magnetic compass, an invention that surfaced independently in China, c. 1000, in Europe, c. 1187, and in Arabia, c. 1200. We also know that Columbus read books and talked to scholars before making his trip. A small personal library of printed books that he took on his travels included *The Book of Marco Polo*, *Pliny's Natural History*, and *Cardinal d'Ailly's Imago Muni*.

Printed books, like the compass, are examples of technological advances. China invented paper early in the 2nd century, and used moveable type in the 11th century, but made no effort to spread these achievements. Instead, in Germany around 1450, Gutenberg, using moveable type in his invention of a printing press, opened up the world of ideas to the common man. Within thirty years, *every* major city in the European states had printing shops.

Today, photocopying, making instant copies using stat-ic electricity, has revolutionized the printing industry. Instantaneous telecommunication, using pulses of electro-magnetic energy, conveys messages, both images and text, from any point in the world to another. Space and distance are no longer barriers in the exchange of infor-mation. In fact, a problem for the 21st century may be too much information rather than too little.

The explosion in telecommunications technology is recent. In 1893 on the 400th anniversary of Columbus's voyages, when the Columbian Exposition in Chicago cele-brated science and technology, the major inventions were the transatlantic cable, the telegraph, and the telephone with its promise of long-distance calls. The 18th century experiments with electricity and electric current had led to these 19th century inventions. You may want to discuss some of these experiments with your class, for it is the understanding of electricity that led to the technology of telecommunication.

To understand today's explosion in communication technology, ask students to name some of the ways peo-ple communicate with one another. Talk about such inventions as the telephone, the cellular phone, the radio, the fax, records, cassettes, CDs, television, cable TV, films, videos, instant replays, video disks, laser disks, and computers. How does each of these technologies allow people to communicate? Which ones let us know people as individuals? As groups? Ask students if they think there is any chance that technology, such as in interactive com-puter games, will replace the traditional book. Discuss the idea that communication technology makes the world both smaller and larger.

Today's technologies also help build worldwide commu-nication networks. Ask students what they know about radio transmission, spectrums, coaxial cables, optical fibers, digital signals, satellites, computers, radio and space telescopes, and space probes. As a class choose one form of communication technology and find out more about its historical development. Students need to know that scientific and technological discoveries are seldom made by one person, but rather come about at times when many people are working on the challenge, often in totally unrelated areas of the world.

Modern information technology has created enormous databanks and information retrieval systems. It is possible to track and collect worldwide data for most areas of human concern. With this information individuals and governments can anticipate supply and demands, and develop solutions in advance of problems.

Columbus made a long voyage across unknown waters in a small boat. Technological advances in transportation have also contributed to advances in communication. Discuss with the students the kinds of changes brought about with the introduction of the horse, the "Iron Horse" of the railroad, the automobile, the airplane, and the jet. Columbus's voyage of more than thirty-three days would be slightly more than three hours on a Concord.

Young people often dream of space voyages to other planets. Though there will be dangers as they journey to the unknown, there will also be links with the earth, thanks to the technology of telecommunication.

ACTIVITIES

Main Concept: Advances in technology allow us to communicate globally.

Weekly Lab
This is a good review of the scientific method. I have students keep records of each type of device they make and notes about how well they work.

Weekly Problem
Answers: 1. 4050 kilometers; 2. 3 hours; 3. 5030.1 miles

Writing for Science
After completing this activity, students should share their results by engaging in classroom discussion.

Challenge
Answers: 1. 960 metric tons; 2. 106 metric tons each

Puzzle
Across: 1. beats, 4. jump, 7. era, 8. move, 9. do, 13. athletes, 14. short, 16. visual; Down: 1. bodies, 2. arm, 3. save, 5. medal, 6. pro, 10. stamina, 11. ask, 13. love.

The Environment and You

BACKGROUND

Environmental awareness was very high in the 1970s. After the shock of the initial energy crunch, peoples' apathy took over again. Earth Day 1990 established the rebirth of environmental awareness. We cannot afford to discontinue the efforts we have made. Its imperative that we make every possible endeavor to continue the changes we are establishing. Continuing educational programs are necessary to ensure that our students learn the importance of making informed choices and of preserving the earth so that today can someday become the past.

When Columbus began the exchange of the five seeds (corn, potatoes, sugar, horse, and disease), he had no idea what the future held. Unlike Columbus, we do know that our future is bleak if we do not make some drastic changes in our lifestyle.

Recycling is one of these necessary changes. Buying recycled products creates a market for recyclables. Reducing the amount of trash that we create also is needed. This can be accomplished by buying products sold in cartons that do not have excess packaging. We can return to reusable plastic containers instead of throw-away plastic bags. Carrying cloth bags to the grocery store will save

having to make the choice between paper or plastic bags. We can require manufacturers to produce products that are not harmful to the environment.

Concerns over the depletion of the rainforest have heightened in recent years. Destruction of this valuable resource has far-reaching impacts, some of which we are not even aware. There are many plants and animals that can live only in the rainforest.

Population growth is again making us more aware of the earth's limitations. With the expected doubling again in 60 years to 10 billion people, the cooperative preservation of resources is imperative. Food and water supplies must be preserved and increased. But the responsibility for doing so rests with each of us. Although we know that the amount of water really will not change, the current supply must be protected from pollution and used wisely.

Finally, students must understand that each individual has the responsibility to care for our fragile planet and that together, we can make a difference.

ACTIVITIES

Main Concept: We must protect our environment. We must educate ourselves on ways to keep the earth healthy.

Weekly Lab
Burying objects in a covered aquarium is similar to putting trash in a plastic garbage bag. Adding one cup of water to the soil is equivalent to rain. The foil and plastic spoon will not decompose in either aquarium. The lettuce and paper in the open aquarium will decompose faster.

Weekly Problem
Answers: 1. 5 1/2; 2. 1 1/2, Wheeling, West Virginia; 3. Great Lakes 4. 4 1/2 5. 6 1/2

Writing for Science
Answers will vary. Have students share their answers. Engage in a classroom discussion about ways students can reduce their daily waste. Listed below are some examples.
1. Use the front and back sides of paper when taking notes.
2. Use glasses and mugs instead of styrofoam.
3. Reuse your grocery bags when you go to the supermarket.
4. Support a bottle bill that establishes a deposit on beverage containers.

Challenge
Have students share their grafts. Start a classroom discussion about these issues.

Puzzle
When students go shopping, they can look for a recycled symbol (three arrows forming a circle) which lets them know that the packaging was made from recycled materials.